The Attributes of God in the Monotheistic Faiths of Judeo-Christian and Islamic Traditions.

The Attributes of God in the Monotheistic Faiths of Judeo-Christian and Islamic Traditions.

HUSEIN KHIMJEE, PH.D.

iUniverse, Inc.
Bloomington

The Attributes of God in the Monotheistic Faiths of Judeo-Christian and Islamic Traditions.

iUniverse books may be ordered through booksellers or by contacting:

iUniverse
1663 Liberty Drive
Bloomington, IN 47403
www.iuniverse.com
1-800-Authors (1-800-288-4677)

ISBN: 978-1-4620-4613-3 (sc)
ISBN: 978-1-4620-4719-2 (ebk)

Printed in the United States of America

iUniverse rev. date: 11/03/2011

Contents

PREFACE

As a university lecturer teaching World Religions, among other religious courses, I have always been fascinated by the common theme that runs through all of the major faiths. There is no faith that I know that does not have teachings of ethics that includes compassion, love, and kindness towards all others. I call it in my introduction to the classes I teach as "one Divine thread" that runs through all the major faiths; whether the faith is a revealed faith like Judaism, Christianity and Islam or whether it is a faith that originated in Asia like Hinduism, Buddhism, Jainism, Confucianism and other faiths originating in that region.

I am particularly fascinated with the discussion of the monotheistic God in the three great monotheistic faiths: Judaism, Christianity, and Islam. These three are put together as the Western Traditions. They are siblings, children of Abraham, who universally called mankind to worship only One God. In the Near East from where these three faiths originate, God has always been referred to with different names like Allah, or Al-ilah, Elah, YHVH and other names. The similarity of these three faiths is truly astounding; particularly when it comes to the discussion of God. One example of this is the similarity in the attributes of the God these three faiths worship.

The other reason for my writing this book is the misunderstanding of Islam portrayed in the media. I was astonished when I heard a lady speaking to a radio host saying that a Muslim God is other than the God that Jews and Christians worship; or also the incident when Pastor Terry Jones burned the Qur'an. My book therefore is to explain, through the attributes of God in all these three faiths, how similar these three faiths are. They worship the same God; some call Him Allah, others call him God, others call him YHVH, or Elah among other names.

One difficulty I encountered was how to explain one major theological difference between Christianity on one side and Judaism and Islam on the other. The difficulty was the status of Jesus. Jews and Muslims do not consider Jesus the Son of God. But while Islam puts Jesus in a very high pedestal as the Messiah, Judaism does not recognize Jesus as the Messiah because Jesus did not fulfill the promise of a Messiah. I therefore decided to include two last chapters in the book describing the status of Jesus in Judaism and Islam.

I must thank my Check In Coordinator, Mars Alma, for her encouragement to finish my manuscript in good time. This helped me greatly to plan not only finishing this work quickly but also to work on the other two books I am working on now.

I am very grateful to my wife and other family members for having put up with me while I was busy writing this book. My particular thanks also to my granddaughter Maryam who very cheerfully helped me type some of my manuscript.

INTRODUCTION

One meaning of the word *God* given in the dictionary is "the Supreme Being considered with reference to a particular attribute: the God of Islam."[1] It can be argued, though, that this is not a totally accurate definition of God simply because God, while correctly stated in the Dictionary as the 'Supreme Being', is not restricted in His particular attribute to only the God of Islam.

God in Islam is the same God of Abraham Jews and Christians worship. Even beyond that, Islam refers to God as the Absolute Sovereign of the universe and the Creator of everything. In this sense, then, He is God of not only the Abrahamic faiths of Judaism, Christianity and Islam but also the God of the universe, lording over everything that is in the heavens and the earth, what is in them and what is between them. God of the universe is the Loving, Compassionate God who nourishes and sustains everything He created and creates. The laws of nature are in His command. He placed the laws so that mankind can explore, and exploit the world, for their progress.

The Arabic name for God is *Allah*. This word too, is not unique to Islam. It is simply an Arabic word used even in pre-Islamic Arabia. Any person familiar with the Middle East will tell you that people of all faiths in the Middle East refer to God as Allah. Some Bibles published in Arabic also use the word Allah referring to God. The uniqueness of the word Allah is explained by Muslim exegetes of the Qur'an. They tell us that the word Allah is derived from the Arabic verb *alaha* (to worship). The noun Allah was originally *al-Ilah*; and takes a meaning of an Arabic participle *al-Ma'aluhu* (one who is worshipped) . . . Quite clearly it has become the proper name of Allah. It was commonly used in this meaning in Arabic long before the Qur'an was revealed . . . other divine names may be used as adjectives for this name; for example, "the Beneficent, the Merciful Allah"; also this name is used as subject of the verbs derived from other divine names; for example, "Allah knew", "Allah had mercy", "Allah gave sustenance" etc. But the word, "Allah" is never used as adjective to any other name, nor is the verb derived from it used to describe other names. It is a clear proof that it is the proper name of God." [2]

This explains the absolute uniqueness of Allah not only in Islam but equally in all the three monotheistic faiths (Judaism, Christianity and Islam). He is described in a frequently recited chapter of the Qur'an as *Ahad*. Another Muslim scholar explains:

"The Qur'an presents its view of God not only in any clearly formulated theological statement or creed, but rather in direct and unambiguous declaration of faith in the one and only God, Creator and Sovereign Lord over all His creation. The following brief *surah* (chapter) known as "Sincere Faith" (*Ikhlas*) or "Divine Oneness" (*Tawhid*) is regarded by Muslims as the clearest explanation of faith.

> *"Say: God, He is One (ahad)*
> *God is the Eternal Refuge (samad)*
> *He neither begets, nor was He begotten*
> *Nor is any one equal to Him."* (Qur'an, 112: 1-4)[3].

The first verse of the *surah* (chapter) above declares God's absolute transcendence in the word '*ahad*' which means "one," not only in number but also in uniqueness. This idea is again affirmed in the final verse: "Nor is there any one (*ahad*) equal to Him." Here too the word *ahad* is used to express God's absolute uniqueness and transcendence over His creation."[4]

This view of God is not different in Judaism as well. A 12th century well-known Jewish scholar, Maimonides, explained the Jewish belief of God like this: "[God], the Cause of all, is one. This does not mean one as in one of a pair, nor one like a species (which encompasses many individuals), nor one as in an object that is made up of many elements, nor as a single simple object that is infinitely divisible. Rather, God is a unity unlike any other possible unity."[5]

There is also yearning in the human being to follow the most supreme authority, to follow God. The question is, though, how does he perceive God? A Christian Scholar tells us that man's perceptions about God will also tell us about his true worldview. It will tell us about his concepts of what good and evil are to him. If we were then to assume that the community he belongs to has a similar worldview, our study could produce interesting conclusions. It will tell us what does the community stands for in their worldview.[6] In a sense, then, it will tell us about the leadership and thinking of the scholars of that community. The leaders and the scholars are the central command system that influences the worldview of their community members. They are the gold of the community. The rest are the laymen. It was Chaucer who said: 'If gold begins to rust, what shall the iron do?' The God perceived by the leaders will be the God perceived by the community members in their worldview. The degree of what they consider ethical living, beneficial to all mankind, will depend on their perception of God the souls are yearning for. Their concept of what is evil and what is good, and as to whether there is any accounting for their deeds will depend on not only their perception of who God is, but also the attributes of God of their perception. Is God, in His essence, unknowable? Inconceivable? Monotheistic faiths of the Jewish, Christian and Islamic traditions do not have much difficulty in perceiving the only God of Abraham they worship. They are the children of Abraham, they are siblings, they worship the same God, yet they have differences.

The major difference that separates the Christian tradition with the Jewish and Islamic traditions is the status of Jesus in the Christian Tradition. Both, Muslims and Jewish reject any notion that God has a son. Islam, while categorically denying this notion, nevertheless, affirms equally strongly that Jesus was a very special Messenger of God, born of virgin Mary, and given special powers to give life to dead, to heal the sick and prophesy about the future events[7] Muslims also categorically reject Jesus was crucified.

Muslims also believe that Jesus was raised alive, is in the heavens alive, and will return in the Last Days to establish the Kingdom of God on the earth. The Qur'an reveals: "And he (Jesus) shall be a Sign (for the coming of) the Hour (of Judgment): therefore have no doubt about the (Hour) but you follow Me: this is the Straight Way" [8] While all the three traditions, the Jewish, the Christian and the Islamic traditions are monotheistic, and they are siblings,[9] the status of Jesus differs in all these three traditions. The status of Jesus is a fascinating account. Therefore, I have included in the book, the last two chapters, that explain the status of Jesus both in the Jewish and in the Islamic traditions.

But does God really exist? The understanding of the Attributes of God can only take proper meaning if God really exists. I am discussing this question in the first chapter and if the readers will find the first chapter interesting, it would be even more interesting to discover what are God's Attributes. This is discussed in the next two chapters, where I have explained how the monotheistic scriptures and their traditions explain the Attributes of God. I have included both, the Jewish and the Christian traditions alone, in a single chapter, "The Attributes of God in the Judeo-Christian Traditions" and as such I have not discussed the concept of Trinity as a separate concept as relating to the Christian tradition. I have elaborated briefly on each Attribute of God in the Judeo-Christian traditions; and in even greater detail in the Islamic tradition. In explaining the Attributes in the Islamic tradition, I have also included the actual Arabic of each Attribute. I have referred to them exactly as is referred to by Muslims, the *Asmaa al-Husna* (the Most Beautiful Names) and have also transliterated each Attribute in English.

CHAPTER ONE:
ABOUT THE EXISTENCE OF GOD.

One of the greatest obstacles in proving the existence of God is that He is unseen. He seems to be detached from all our sensual perceptions. Not only can we not see Him with our eyes or hear Him with our ears, we cannot feel Him anywhere by touching Him. Yet the monotheistic scriptures tell us that not only He is the existing God, He is fully involved in our daily lives; that although we cannot see Him, He sees us, He is as close to us as our own jugular vein[10]. The other obstacle in discussing the existence of God is the fear of idolatry. We cannot imagine Him in our minds as a Being of any kind, for doing so would mean we have created His image in our minds. Scriptures tell us that man was created in the image of God. In the Qur'an we read that God blew of His own Spirit into man and that He created man with His own two Hands. Can we then not imagine God to be a man-like figure Himself? The answer given by all monotheists is of course "No", because then God would become something captured in the imagination of our minds and would be no more than an idol. This would be blasphemous. Also any spontaneous imagination of God could also lead one theorizing God as a mythological Being. Close scrutiny of such theorization reveals a creation of something from objects and things we are already familiar with in our surroundings. It would be mixing and matching of things we are familiar with and give it a new shape of a mythological being. To believe in monotheistic God is to believe in God who is "like nothing else"[11] To believe in God is to believe that everything has been created *ex-nihillo* and that it was created in time and has been given a life-cycle of its own. In the end, its demise is certain. God is the only One who is ever-lasting. God is the only One who is not affected by time. God is a self-existing Being, this belief is "not a wisp of dry doctrine, academic and remote; it is in fact as near as our breath and as practical as the latest surgical technique"[12] It is interesting that prophets, as mouthpieces of God, articulated as it was revealed to them. The anthropomorphic terms are only meant to simplify understanding for the human mind. God reveals Himself as the one who Sees, who Hears, who Knows all, but it would be blasphemy to imagine

Him as a Being like any of His other creation. The scriptures explained and taught in parables.

The problem of unseen is not new. Thinkers have philosophized this in different ways and have concluded that the reality of unseen cannot be discarded; that the only real things are not those that we can prove by our sensual perceptions; that if a thing is not seen, it certainly does not mean that it is not there or that it does not exist. As a matter of fact, what we can prove through our sensual perceptions is also not always true. The twinkling stars we see with our eyes are not really twinkling. They appear so, because the light they emit passes through the atmosphere in the space distorting their image. On a hot day, our eyes may see at a distance the actual mass body of collected water but it turns out to be only a mirage. The rising moon on the horizon appears larger than when it is overhead. In reality, it should appear larger when it is overhead. Our sensual perceptions give us distorted view. The argument presented by the thinkers is also that sensual perceptions do not necessarily lead us to any definite conclusions. For example, take an egg. We can see an egg with our eyes, we can feel it when we touch it, we can taste it when we eat it, and we can smell it when it is cooked. All our sensual perceptions conclude for us that it is an egg. Our sensual perceptions, however, can definitely not conclude which came first, the egg or the hen! We must use our rational perceptions to arrive at some sort of conclusion. For a secularist or an atheist, it was merely an accident in history. If this was so, why is there no accident in the symmetry and the perfectness in the nutrients of an egg. For a monotheist, it was the Creator, it was God who created first the hen and the instincts to mate and to incubate and to pro-create.

Philosophers in the distant past have explained the best. Plato was troubled by the illusory world. He argued the sensual perceptions are deceiving. What we see are only the shadows of the real thing. They are only illusions. The real thing is unseen. Plato explained this in Theory of Forms. This theory explains that the objects we see are only the 'shadows' of the real Form. Plato explained this in his 'Analogy of a Cave'. In this cave, human beings are seated, chained in such a way that they cannot even move their necks. They can look only straight. Behind them, at a distance is raging fire. Between the fire and where these human beings are seated, is a walkway on which people are passing, some of them carrying different objects. The shadows of these people walking and the objects they are carrying is carried in front of the chained human beings. All what they see are the shadows of people walking and the shadows of objects.

These chained human beings have never looked at anything else. To them, these shadows are the real things. Plato then shows one of these chained human beings is released and for the first time in his life, he can turn his neck to look sideways and sees behind him for the first time, the fire raging at the distance and people walking on the walkway. He is dazzled at first and then thinks the actual people walking on the walkway are not real. The real to him were the shadows he was used to throughout his early life when he was chained. This man is now taken outside of the cave and for the first time he sees the Sun in the sky. He is in absolute shock only to realize that what he was seeing in his earlier life, when he was chained, was not real. It was only the illusion. He is now illumined in his learning. He understood what he thought was real when he was chained was only a passing phenomenon. It was deceiving. He now feels he has the duty to teach others who are still chained in their wretched condition. He runs down into the cave and explains the reality to his chained mates. He explains to them that what they are accustomed to seeing is not real. It is all illusory . . . but they only laugh at him.

Plato used the Sun as his supreme example to explain the reality. Abraham, the patriarchal figure of the monotheistic faiths of Judaism, Christianity and Islam, also used the Sun as one of the examples, but showed the Sun only as one of the created planets that eventually set at the end of the day. Abraham showed his idols and planets worshipping community that the only Being worthy of worship is Allah, who is the Creator of not only the planets in the heavens but everything else; and that everything must in the end perish. This example is given in the Qur'an. Abraham wants to teach his community. He tells them pointing to the star in the darkness of the night, "*This is my Lord*". But when the star set, he said, "*I do not love those that set*". Then when he saw the moon rising in splendor, he said, "*This is my Lord.*" But when the moon set, he said, "*Unless my Lord guides me, I shall surely be among those who go astray.*" When he saw the sun rising in splendor, he said, "*This is my Lord; this is the greatest (of all).*" But when the sun set, he said, "*O my people! I am indeed free from your (guilt) of giving partners to God. For me, I have set my face, firmly and truly, toward Him Who created the heavens and the earth, and I shall never give partners to God.*"[13] The Qur'an reveals many examples and parables Abraham used to teach his community about the reality of the existence of God. The Qur'an refers Abraham as the *Imam an-Naas* (the leader of mankind) The Qur'an itself has several parables explaining through signs in the nature the reality of the Creator. The Qur'an asks mankind to look around them, to ponder, to think.

"Do they not see how are camels created?
And how is the heavens raised?
And how are the mountains fixed firm?
And how the earth is spread out?"[14]

The question of the reality of unseen was thought of by other cultures as well. In the Far East, Confucius thought of the same. In his Analects we read a disciple of Confucius saying that his Master always said that 'The real things were only those that could not be seen and the real sounds were only those that could not be heard.[15]

In India, too, the sages have come to the same conclusions as Plato and Confucius. Indian scriptures have a wonderful story. A sage is explaining to his rebellious son about the reality of the existence of God. The father asks his son to get a clay cup full of water, and put some salt into it. He tells his son to come back the next morning. When the son returns in the morning, he is asked to take out the salt from the water. The son searches for it, but cannot find it, because the salt had already dissolved. His father asked him to taste the water. The son tasted the water at the top, in the middle, and at the bottom. When asked how the water tasted, the son replied that it tasted salty. His father told him "You do not see what is in the water but you can taste it. That shows that the salt does exist. In the same way, even though you cannot see God, He is indeed there. God, where everything comes from, and merges in is everything in the universe. That truth is all of us. That thou art, my son![16]The Hindu tradition, although not monotheistic, its scriptures are filled with several anecdotes pointing to the reality of the existence of God.

Islamic literature promotes the notion of using one's intellect to arrive at the reality of the existence of God. In one of their books, we read:
"We believe that Allah has endowed us with the faculty of the intellect (`aql), and that He has ordered us to ponder over His creation, noting with care the signs of His Power and His Glory throughout the entire universe as well as within ourselves. It is stated in the Qur'an:

> *"We shall show them Our signs on the horizons and in themselves, till it is clear to them that it is the Truth"* (41: 43)

Allah has shown His disapproval of those who blindly follow the ways of those who were before them:

> *"They say "No, but we will follow such things as we found our father doing." What! And if their fathers had no understanding of anything.* (2:170); and He has shown dislike for those who follow nothing but their own personal whims: *"They follow naught but their opinion"* (6:117).

Indeed, our intellect forces us to reflect upon Creation so as to know the Creator of the universe, just as it makes it necessary for us to examine the claims of someone to prophet hood and to consider the truth of his miracles. It is not correct to accept the ideas of someone without criticism, even if that person has the gift of great knowledge or holds an esteemed position. The reason that the Qur'an has urged us to reflect upon Creation and to study the natural world and acquire knowledge is so that it may confirm in us mankind's instinctual freedom of thought upon which all sages are in agreement . . ."[17]

In his book, *Let Me See Thy Glory: A Study of the Attributes of God,* Robert Deffinbaugh tells us that "The way to "see" God is to come to know Him through a study of His character as revealed in the Scriptures.

Dr. Kenneth Boa, a Christian scholar engaged in a ministry of evangelism and discipleship explains the existence of God by giving what he calls 'four incontrovertible features of the world' to prove God's existence:

1. The existence of the universe and therefore it had to have a beginning; a contingency that requires some kind of causality
2. The fine-tuning of cosmos and all creations that has to have a 'Fine Tuner'
3. The origin of life itself
4. The genetic-code, where each cell has six feet of DNA rich in information. It is a language in itself that has its own alphabets, words, syntax and intentionality.

Dr. Boa is also quoting Psalm 19 as a fundamental revelation in understanding the existence of God through the signs in nature. The workings of God and His love is also seen in Romans 1.

It would be categorical error to ask who created God. God is not a created being. God is uncreated, boundless (see www.kenboa.org).

No man can see God and live (Exodus 33:20). No man has seen God at any time (John 1:18). Men have "seen" God partially at various times when He has appeared in various forms (see Exodus 24:9-11; 33:17-34:7;

Isaiah 6:5). In every instance when God manifested Himself visibly to men, there is only a partial revelation of His glory, for man could no more look upon the full display of God's splendor than one can look directly into the sun. We are among those who have not "seen" our LORD (John 20:29; 1 Peter 1:8). Our grasp of the nature of God . . . must be limited to what the Scriptures teach concerning His teaching . . . In the final analysis, we can "see" and know God through the Scriptures as they reveal His character to us.[18]

In one very interesting incident revealed in the Qur'an we see Moses asking God to show Himself to Moses. This was on the Mount Sinai when Moses went up to receive the Law. The conversation is revealed in the Qur'an: *"When Moses came to the place appointed by Us, and his Lord addressed him, he said: "O my Lord! Show (Thyself) to me, that I may look upon Thee." God said: "By no means can you see Me (direct); but look upon the mount; if it abide in its place, then shall you see Me." When his Lord manifested His glory on the Mount, He made it as dust, and Moses fell down in a swoon. When he recovered his senses he said: "Glory to You! To You I turn in repentance, and I am the first to believe."*[19]

In monotheistic faiths, as we will see in the chapters that follow, God not only exists, He is the only true Sovereign of the heavens and the earth, what is in them and what is between them. There is no other partner in His Sovereignty. Any other notion about God can lead to idolatry. Tozer in his book, *The Knowledge of the Holy* tells us that "the idolatrous heart assumes that God is other than He is . . . Let us beware lest we in our pride accept the erroneous notion that idolatry consists only in kneeling before visible objects of adoration, and that civilized peoples are therefore free from it. The essence of idolatry is the entertainment of thoughts about God that are unworthy of Him."[20]

God exists, but what is He like? Tozer tells us that if by that question we mean "What is God like in *Himself?* There is no answer. If we mean 'what has God disclosed *about Himself* that the reverent reason can comprehend?' there is . . . an answer both full and satisfying. For while the name of God is secret and His essential nature incomprehensible, He in condescending love has by revelation declared certain things to be true to Himself. These we call His attributes".[21]

But it is also essential to remember that the attribute is not a part of God. Neither can we call the attribute of God a *quality* of God; or any such adjective we give when describing created things. God is not a created Being and He does not owe His Being to anyone. Neither is He divisible because all His attributes are in unison with His Being. "The harmony of His being is the result not of a perfect balance of parts but of the absence of parts. Between His attributes no contradiction can exist. He need not suspend one to exercise another, for in Him all attributes are one . . . He does not divide Himself to perform a work, but works in the total unity of His being".[22]

The first Imam of Shi`a Muslims, and among the 'Rightly Guided Caliphs' of all Muslims, Imam Ali explains:

"The foremost in religion is the acknowledgment of Him, the perfection of acknowledging Him is to testify Him, the perfection of testifying Him is to believe in His One-ness, the perfection of believing in His One-ness is to regard Him Pure, and the perfection of His purity is to deny Him attributes (as if to limit Him),because every attribute is a proof that it is different from that to which it is attributed and everything to which something is attributed is different from the attribute. Thus whoever attaches attributes to Allah recognizes His like, and who recognizes His like regards Him two; and who regards Him two recognizes parts of Him; and who recognizes parts of Him mistook Him; and who mistook Him pointed at Him; and who pointed at Him admitted limitations to Him; and who admitted limitations for Him numbered Him".

Imam Ali goes on to explain that whoever said in what is He, held that God is contained in something. God is a Being but not through a phenomenon of coming into being. He exists but not from non-existence. He is as close to our jugular vein but not in the sense of physical nearness. God is different from everything but not in physical separation. In His actions, He does not need any instruments. There are no connotations of movements. God is the only One God. He is such that there is none with whom He may keep company or whom He may miss in his absence.

(See Imam `Ali, Nahj al-Blaagha:Sermons, Letters and Sayings, Tr. Syed Ali Raza, Karachi, 1971), pp,20-23.

CHAPTER TWO:
THE ATTRIBUTES OF GOD IN THE JUDEO-CHRISTIAN TRADITIONS.

Like Islam, the fundamental principle in the Jewish and the Christian traditions is the belief in the existence of one and only God. In the Old Testament, God is referred to by at least 21 names.

Adonai[23]	Jehovah-Rapha
Elohim[24]	Jehovah—Sabaoth
El (the Strong One)	Jehovah-Mekaddishkem
El-Roi	Jehovah-Shalom
El Elohe Yisrael	Jehovah-Nissi
El Shaddai	Jehovah-Shammah
El Elyon	Jehovah Tsidkenu
El Olam	Jehovah[26]
Immanuel[25]	Yah or Jah
Jehovah Jireh	YHVH
Jehovah-Rohi (Jehovah Rohi)	

The most frequently used name of God in the Hebrew Bible is YHVH. It is freely and frequently used and appears in the Hebrew Bible more than 7000 times[27]

But the first name used for God in the Bible is 'Elohim'. Exegetes tell us that the name 'Elohim' appears over 2000 times. What is interesting about the name "Elohim" is that it appears attached with an attribute of God. This should not suggest any duality of God. Rather, it emphasizes even more the unique oneness of God. The attached attribute with the name "Elohim" is not a separate entity. It is a qualifying attribute of "Elohim" and is inherent and is part of the unique one God. "Elohim" also means 'power' and 'strength'. Again, this does not mean that God had to train Himself to acquire power and strength. He is the sole Creator of the heavens and the earth. The total singular power and total strength through which He creates and maintains all affairs and all His other attributes are not something that are acquired. His power and His strength and all other attributes He has are eternal with Him. As explained above, He is not like any other thing that can be captured in human imagination. The uniqueness of this belief is also that God is not the mythological being; neither is He detached from the everyday life of His creation. Rather, He is the active God, the Ever-living. Ever-subsisting. He is the Power and the Strength; at the same time it gives a great comfort to believers to know that He is all-Merciful, all-Compassionate God. He has the absolute authority over everything; yet He is not corrupt. He is the Just God. He is not aloof from His creation. Neither has He created the heavens and the earth without any purpose. Through His Power and Strength, He created heavens and the earth, and everything else, *ex-nihillo.* Genesis 1:1 tells us: "In the beginning Elohim created the heaven and the earth." The attributes given after his name are therefore only the adjectives qualifying His singular quality. The other interesting thing to understand about monotheistic God is that He is a singular God. Since God is not indivisible, all the qualities referred to in His attributes are combined in Him at one and the same time. The description given in the Bible of all His names above, also gives His attributes. Let us look at some of the names I have shown above and the attributes attached to these names in the Bible. He is described in the scripture as YHVH. It simply means "to be" or "I AM". God said to Moses at the Burning Bush that He (God) was what He was, "I am who I am." At that point, Bible tells us that God instructed Moses to proclaim this fact to the children of Israel, and to tell them that God has sent Moses to tell them this:

"I AM has sent me to you . . . this is My eternal name, and this is how I am to be recalled for all generations'" (Exodus 3:14-15).

This is the ultimate example of the Absoluteness of God. He is who He is, the only God. He is the Beginning and the Ending. There is none equal to Him. This is the fundamental belief of the three great monotheistic faiths, the Jewish, the Christian and the Islamic traditions. For the Jews, this name is not to be pronounced in vain (Exodus, 20:7); and Jews would not pronounce this. Instead, they would prefer to use Adonai. The Hebrew Bible, though, uses YHVH freely and describes further, with it, the attributes of God.

Here are some examples from the Hebrew Bible.

YHVH Elohim—LORD God:
"These are the generations of the heavens and the earth when they were created in the day that the LORD God made the earth and the heavens" (Genesis 2:4).

YHVH O'saynu—The LORD our Maker:
"O come let us worship and bow down, let us kneel before the LORD, our Maker !"(Psalm 95:6).

YHVH M'kadesh—The LORD Who Makes Holy:
"Then the nations will know that I the LORD sanctify Israel, when my sanctuary is in the midst of them evermore" (Ezekiel 37:28).

YHVH Nissi—The LORD My Banner:And Moses built an altar and called the name for it, The LORD is my banner". (Exodus 17:15).

YHVH Shalom—The LORD Of Peace:
Then Gideon built an altar there to the LORD, and called it, The LORD of Peace". (Judges 6:24).

YHVH Tzidkaynu—The LORD Our Righteousness:
"In those days Judah will be saved and Jerusalem will dwell securely. And this is the name by which it will be called: 'The LORD is our righteousness". (Jeremiah 33:16)

ELOHIM (or ELOHAY):
Elohay Selichot—God Of Forgiveness:
". . . Thou art a God ready to forgive, gracious and merciful, slow to anger and abounding in steadfast love . . ."(Nehemiah 9:17).

Elohay Kedem—God of the Beginning:
". . . The Eternal God is your dwelling place and underneath are the everlasting arms . . ."(Deuteronomy 33:27).

Elohay Mishpat—God Of Justice:
"For the LORD is a God of justice . . ." (Isaiah 30:18).

Elohay Mikarov—God Who Is Near:

"Am I a God at hand, says the LORD, and not a God afar off?"(Jeremiah 23:23).

Elohay Mauzi—God Of My Strength:
"For thou art the God in whom I take refuge . . ."(Psalm 43:2).

Elohay Tehilati—God Of My Praise:
"Be not silent, O God of my praise!" (Psalm 109:1).

Elohay Yishi—God Of My Salvation:
". . . and exalted be the God of my salvation . . ."(Psalm 18:46).

Elohim Kedoshim—Holy God:
". . . For I the LORD your God am holy . . ."(Leviticus 19:2), and ". . . Joshua said to the people, "You cannot serve the LORD; for he is a holy God . . . (Joshua 24:19).

Elohim Chaiyim—Living God:
"But the LORD is the true God; he is the living God and the everlasting King." (Jeremiah 10:10).

Elohay Elohim—God Of Gods:
"For the LORD your God is God of gods and LORD of LORDs . . ."(Deuteronomy 10:17).

Elohay Marom—God Of Heights:
"With what shall I come before the LORD, and bow myself before God on the high?(Micah 6:6).

Among many other of His attributes, Psalm also tells us He is our Shepherd, He is our LORD. It is He who is the Creator. Therefore, "The heavens are telling the glory of God; and the firmament proclaims His handiwork. Day to day pours forth speech, and night to night declares knowledge" (Psalm Ch.19). It also tells: "Know that the LORD is God. It is He that made us, and we are His, we are His people, and the sheep of His pasture. Enter His gates with thanksgiving, and His courts with praise! Give thanks to Him, and bless His name! For the LORD is Good; His steadfast love endures forever, and His faithfulness continues through all generations." (Psalm Ch. 100:2-5)

EL: Adjectives are used also with His other name, 'El". These are Attributes of God. He is:

El HaNe'eman—The Faithful God:
"Know therefore that the LORD your God is God, the faithful God . . ."(Deuteronomy 7:9).

El HaGadol—The Great God:
"For the LORD your God is God of gods, and Lord of lords, the great, the mighty . . . and takes no bribe", (Deuteronomy 10:17). Other examples with the Attributes of God beginning with the article 'El' are:
ElHaKadosh—The Holy God:
"But the LORD of hosts is exalted in justice and the Holy God shows himself holy in righteousness". (Isaiah 5:16).

El Yisrael—The God Of Israel:
". . . God in his sanctuary, the God of Israel, he gives power and strength to his people, Blessed be God!" (Psalm 68:35).

El HaShamayim—The God Of The Heavens:
"O give thanks to the God of heaven, for his steadfast lave endures forever". (Psalm 136:26).

El De'ot—The God Of Knowledge:
"Talk no more so very proudly, let not arrogance come from your mouth; for the LORD is a God of knowledge, and by him actions are weighed". (1 Sam 2:3).

El Emet—The God of Truth:
"Thou hatest those who pay regards to vain idols; but I trust in the LORD". (Psalm 31:6).

El Yeshuati—The God Of My Salvation:
"Behold, God is my salvation; I will trust, and will not be afraid; for the LORD GOD is my strength and my song, and he has become my salvation". (Isaiah 12:2).

El Elyon—The Most High God:
"And Melchiz'edek kingof Salem brought out bread and wine; he was priest of God Most High".(Genesis 14:18).

Immanu El—God Is With Us:
"Therefore the Lord himself will give you a sign. Behold, a young woman shall conceive and bear a son, and shall call his name Immanu El (Isaiah 7:14).

El Olam—The God Of Eternity
"Abraham planted a tamarisk tree in Beer-sheba, and called there on the name of the LORD, the Everlasting God".(Genesis 21:33).

El Echad—The One God:
Have we not all one father? Has not one God created us? Why then are we faithless to one another, profaning the covenant of our fathers?" (Malachi 2:10).

ELAH isThe Hebrew Bible uses this name about 70 times. Adjectives are added to this to again show more Attributes of God. In Ezra, for example, we find these Attributes:

Elah Sh'maya—God of Heaven:
"Whatever is commanded by the God of heaven . . ."(Ezra 7:23).

Elah Sh'maya V'Arah—God of Heaven and Earth:
"We are the servants of the God of heaven and earth . . ."(Ezra 5:11).

Elah Yerush'lem—God of Jerusalem:
". . . You shall deliver before the God of Jerusalem . . ."(Ezra 7:19).

Elah Yisrael—God of Israel:
". . . prophesied to the Jews who were in Judah and Jerusalem, in the name of the God of Israel who was over them . . ." (Ezra 5:1)

Reading through both, the Hebrew Bible (The Old Testament) and the New Testament one can see immediately that God is mentioned with several of His attributes. Some examples, revealed in both the Old Testament and the New Testament, are that God is the true Sovereign, God is the Spirit, God is the Self-existent, God is the Perfect, God is the Creator, God is the Omnipresent, God is the Omnipotent, God is the Omniscient, It is God who gives the Life and Death, God is the Eternal, God is the Immutable, God is the Holy, God is the Good, God is the Judge, God is the Righteous, God is the Love. The scriptures expound these attributes in the stories and parables they reveal.

Here is a small example.

God is the Absolute Sovereign

God is the absolute Sovereign of the Universe. He rules over all.
In the Hebrew Bible, in Psalm 103:19 and in 135:6 we read:

"The LORD has established his throne in the heavens, and his kingdom rules over all".
"Whatever the LORD pleases He does, in the heaven and on earth, in the seas and all deeps. He it is who makes the clouds rise at the end of the earth, who makes lightening for the rain and brings forth the wind from his storehouses."

There are similar passages scattered throughout the Bible attributing all Sovereignty belonging only to God.

In the New Testament, one of my favorite passage is Acts 17:24-29 which reveals:

"The God who made the world and everything in it, being Lord of heaven and earth, does not live in shrines made by man, nor is he served by human hands, as though he needed anything, since he himself gives to all men life and breath and everything. And he made from every nation of men to live on all the face of the earth, having determined allotted periods and the boundaries of their habitation, that they should seek God, in the hope that they might feel after him and find him. Yet he is not far from each one of us, for 'In him we live and move and have our being'.

This passage in the New Testament shows not only the attribute of absolute Sovereignty of God over everything in the universe, but it also shows God's attribute as the one who gives life and death in a period determined only by God alone. Therefore, there has to be a reason why are we here. Our deeds have to be judged by our righteousness. God is therefore the ultimate Judge of all our deeds.

God is the Just
God as the ultimate Judge of all our deeds is a Just God. And on the fixed Day mankind will be fully judged in their righteousness. Not a soul will be wronged. In an interesting event we read in the New Testament, Paul is

shown addressing men of Athens, whom he saw worshipping idols. Paul said that mankind should not think God is like gold, or silver or stone. This would be only the representation of art or imagination of man. God has overlooked the ignorance of man involved in such idolatry, but in the advent of Jesus it is required for mankind to repent; because God has certainly fixed a day for mankind to be judged in their righteousness. (Acts 17:29)

God is the Spirit.

God cannot be imagined as something akin to what He has created. As explained above, any such imagination leads only to idolatry. In the Hebrew Bible, we read in Genesis 1:1-2, "In the beginning God created the heavens and the earth. The earth was without form and void, and darkness was upon the face of the deep; and the Spirit of God was moving over the face of the waters." In the New Testament, we read in John 4:24, "God is spirit, and those who worship him, must worship him in spirit and truth." God is therefore invisible and can never be envisioned in our imagination.

God is the Self-existent

Exodus 3:13-14 shows without any ambiguity that God is Self-existant. Then Moses said to God, "If I come to the people of Israel and say to them, 'The God of your fathers has sent me to you,' and they ask me, 'what is His name'?' what shall I say to them? God said to Moses, "I AM WHO I AM" AND He said, "say this to the people of Israel, I AM has sent me to you".

God is the Creator

A beautiful hymn, Psalm 19:1, reads, "The heavens are telling the glory of God; and the firmament proclaims his handiwork." Also in 24:1-2, "The earth is the LORD'S and the fullness thereof, the world and those who dwell therein; for he has founded it upon the seas, and established it upon the rivers".

In the New Testament, we read in Acts 14:15, "Men, why are you doing this? We also are men, of like nature with you, and bring you the good news, that you should turn from these vain things to a living God who made the heavens and the earth and the sea and all that is in them".

God is the Perfect

In Psalm 19:7-9 we read, "The law of the LORD is perfect, reviving the soul; the testimony of the LORD is sure, making wise the simple; the precepts of the LORD are right, rejoicing the heart; the commandment of the LORD is pure, enlightening the eyes'.

In the New Testament, Romans 12:2 tells us that the perfectness can be achieved by being transformed by the renewal of our mind and realizing God is good and perfect, "Do not be conformed to this world, but be transformed by the renewal of your mind, that you may prove what is the will of God, what is good and acceptable and perfect".

God is the Giver of Life and Death

It is God who gives life. It is also He who gives death. Life is therefore totally dependent on Him.

Psalms 36:9 reveals: "For with thee is the fountain of life;; in thy light do we see light". Also Daniel 5:23 tells us that our breath is in the hands of God and that the real honor belongs to Him alone; "but you have lifted up yourself against the Lord of heaven; and the vessels of his house have been brought in before you, and you and your lords, your wives, and your concubines have drunk wine from them; and you have praised the gods of silver and gold, of bronze, iron, wood, and stone, which do not see or hear or know, but the God in whose hand is your breath, and whose are all your ways, you have not honored".

God is the Infinite

God cannot have any boundaries limiting Him in any way. His Knowledge, His Power and all His other attributes are absolute and limitless. His Compassion, Mercy and Love knows no bounds. When we as human beings think, our thinking has limited notions. We know things through our sensual perceptions and make conclusions intelligently combining our sensual perceptions with our rational perceptions. God does not go through this process. His knowledge is eternal. Our conclusions are derived from our thinking, our witnessing things and our experiences. God is above, high above all this. A preacher explained this nicely; when we are on the earth, we can see only as far as our vision goes, but when we fly and look below through the window of an airplane, we see much more. The limit of our vision expands because we are above and there are no obstructions. But God is above everything else and can see everything in a way that is limitless. The preacher still did not explain completely. Even from the airplane or a spacecraft, our vision is still limited. For God, there is no hindrance of any kind. His infinitude is incomprehensible simply because a finite cannot fully understand the infinite. A scholar once explained by saying that an object weighing, let us say, one kilogram, can never be able to understand or explain what it means to be an object weighing one ton!

God is the Immutable

Everything that we see around us is created and has a life-cycle of its own. It begins to degenerate and depreciate until it runs off its life-cycle. This is not so with God. He does not mutate and does not differ in any way, shape or form. As a matter of fact, we cannot even think in the terms of Almighty God having any shape or form. A shape or size can mutate; God is immutable.

In his book, The Knowledge of the Holy, A. W. Tozer describes several attributes of God. Tozer wrote the book mainly for his Christian audience lamenting at what he saw "the Christian conception of God current in these middle years of the twentieth century is so decadent as to be utterly beneath the dignity of the Most High God and actually to constitute for professed believers something amounting to a moral calamity. All the problems of heaven and earth, though they were to confront us together and at once, would be nothing compared with the overwhelming problem of God: That He is; what He is like; and what we as moral beings must do about Him".[28]

Tozer wanted Christians to come to the right belief about God so that they could be relieved of what he calls "ten thousand temporal problems . . . but even if the multiple burdens of time may be lifted from him, the one mighty single burden of eternity begins to press down upon him with a weight more crushing than all the woes of the world piled one upon another. That mighty burden is his obligation to God."[29] It is to relieve Christians from this burden, and to prevent any idolatrous notion of God, Tozer shows that the status of the Almighty God of Abraham can be fully understood through His attributes. Tozer shows that God is: Self-Sufficient, Eternal, Infinite, Immutable, Omnipotent, Omniscient, Omnipresent, Transcendent, Wise, Faithful, Good, Gracious, Holy, Sovereign, Just, Loving, Good and Merciful. Tozer ties God's mercy eventually to the advent of Jesus.

The Jewish and the Islamic traditions show the compassion and mercy of God through the prophets of God and through the promise of mercy when one repents and reforms from committing sins. Interestingly, Muslims view Jesus as a very special prophet and believe he will return in the last days; and will establish the Kingdom of God in which love and mercy will prevail with equity and justice for all. The difference being that Jesus will proclaim his status as only the Messenger and slave of God. In the Islamic tradition, all prophets were Muslims (those who submitted themselves totally to the Will of One God and believed that there is no other god or gods).

Tozer's focus, as a faithful Christian himself, is solely upon the Christian community. Tozer hopes that "any intensified knowledge of God will soon begin to affect those around us in the Christian community"

God is, in all monotheistic traditions, above all categories of time and space, form and number, or any other material or temporal attributions. Yet He can be known through His Attributes.

In the Islamic tradition, the attributes of Allah are referred to in the Qur'an, as the Asma` al-Husna, Allah's most beautiful Names. It is to this now that I turn.

CHAPTER THREE:
THE ATTRIBUTES OF ALLAH (GOD) IN THE ISLAMIC TRADITION:
THE *ASMAA AL-HUSNA* OR THE MOST BEAUTIFUL NAMES.

Allah[30], High and Exalted is He, reveals Himself in the Qur'an like this:

> *Allah, there is no god but He[31], the Living, the Self-subsisting,*
> *Eternal. No slumber can seize Him nor sleep. To Him belongs*
> *whatever is in the heavens and the earth. Who is it who can*
> *intercede with Him unless He permits? He knows what is ahead*
> *of them and what is behind them And no one can comprehend*
> *His knowledge about anything except as He wishes. His Throne*
> *extends over the heavens and the earth; protection of both (the*
> *heavens and the earth) does not tire Him; and He is the Exalted,*
> *the Mighty[32].*

This Verse in the Qur'an, referred to as the "Verse of the Throne" sums up the Majesty, the Grandeur, the Omnipotence, the Absoluteness and the Power of Allah. His Majesty is also summed up in another wonderful passage in the Qur'an:

> *Whatever is in the heavens and on earth declares*
> *The Praises and Glorifies Allah for He is the*
> *Exalted in Might, the Wise.*
> *To Him belongs the dominions of the heavens and*
> *The earth. It is He who gives Life and Death; and*
> *He has Power over all things.*
> *He is the First and the Last, the Evident and the Immanent:*
> *And He has Knowledge of all things.*
> *He it is who created the heavens and the earth in six Days,*
> *And is moreover firmly established on the Throne. He*
> *Knows what enters within the earth and what comes forth*
> *Out of it, what comes down from heaven and what mounts up to it.*

And He is with you wheresoever you may be.
And Allah sees well all that you do.
To Him belongs the dominion of the heavens and the earth:
And all affairs are referred back to Allah. He merges Night into
Day, and He merges Day into Night. He has full knowledge of
the secrets of (all) hearts.[33]

Another chapter in the Qur'an sums up the true essence of Allah in the Islamic belief. Muslims recite this chapter almost everyday and is part of their fundamental belief about who God truly is:

In the name of Allah, the Beneficent, the Merciful.
Say: He is Allah the One and Only;
Allah the Eternal, Absolute;
He begets not, nor is He begotten;
And there is none like unto Him.[34]

What we see from the above passages, revealed in the Qur'an, are several attributes of Allah. These and all other attributes of Allah have been classified by Muslim theologians into three categories:

1. The attributes that indicate all the Divine perfections in Allah; of His total knowledge of everything; of His total mercy and His total power and strength; and also attributes that show complete negation of any imperfection and deficiency. They indicate that Allah does not beget nor is He begotten; that He does not have any physical body that one can visualize as having a life cycle of its own, that would grow and finally die. Allah is Eternal. Life and death are not the phenomena that affect Him. The attributes also show that Allah is not confined to any place.
2. The attributes that indicate Allah's Divine Essence. Allah does not depend on any other being. He does not depend on any bestower to bestow power or life or anything else.
3. The attributes that show His Divine acts and the relationship between Him and His creatures. The attributes show Allah is forgiving, loving, caring, protecting, and a guiding God to His creatures.

The name *Allah* is His Own self, this name fully reflects His *Dhaat* (Essence). This name, including its variations is used 2816 times in the Qur'an. The other names to describe Him are *Ilah*, mentioned 120 times, and the word *Rabb*, mentioned 963 times. The most frequently used word to denote God in the Qur'an is *Allah*.[35]

The name *Allah* is also referred to as *al-ism al—a`azam*, the Greatest Name, and in its Essence, it contains all the divine attributes of God, it is the sign of His Essence and is the cause of all existence. Nothing else can assume this name. This name belongs only to Allah Himself. The Qur'an reveals about the uniqueness of this name. We read from the Qur'an:

> *Lord of the Heavens and of the Earth, and of all that is between them: So worship Him, and be constant and patient in His worship. Do you Know of any who is worthy of the same name as He?*[36]

The name *Allah* contains five meanings, qualities that indicate the non-resemblance of Allah to anything else. These are:

Qidam. He is before the before. He did not become. He always was.
Baqa. He is after the after, the Eternal; He always will be.

Wahdaniyyah. He is unique, without any partner, without resemblance, the cause of all. Everything is in need of Him and all came into existence by His Command, "Be!" and must reach the end of their life by His Command.

Mukhalafatun lil-hawadith. He is the Creator, and He bears no resemblance to the created.

Qiyam bi-nafsihi. He is self-existent, does not need anybody for His existence. He is without any needs.

Further, Allah is perfection. The extent of His perfection is infinite. The greatest name, *Allah*, contains eight essentials indicating His perfection. He is Ever-living; He is All-knowing; He is All-Hearing, He is All-Seeing; All will is His; All Power is His; All existence and actions depend upon Him; The word, all that is said and taught, is His.[37] Allah's Grandeur and Majesty can be seen beautifully in His attributes. In the Qur'an, believers are asked to invoke Allah by these names: The Qur'an tells the believers,

> *"The most beautiful names belong to Allah: so call on Him by them . . ."*[9]

In this Chapter, I will first mention the 99 attributes of Allah invoked in Islam. This should not be taken to mean that Allah's total attributes in Islam are limited to only 99. There are several variations derived from these attributes alone and therefore the attributes of Allah are unlimited in number and each name is a source of great comfort to Muslims as each name is considered divine and is invoked in many occasions. As already mentioned above, the Qur'an itself encourages to call upon Allah by His names, the *Asma` al-Husna*. I will name each of these 99 divine attributes and give a brief explanation of each of these attributes in the pages that follow. The 99 Attributes of Allah are:

1. *Ar Rahmanu*
   The All-Merciful
2. *Ar Rahimu*
   The Beneficent
3. *Al Maliku*
   The Sovereign Lord
4. *Al Quddusu*
   The Holy
5. *As Salaamu*
   The Source of Peace
6. *Al Mu'minu*
   The Guardian of Faith
7. *Al Muhayminu*
   The Protector
8. *Al `Azizu*
   The Mighty
9. *Al Jabbaru*
   The Compeller
10. *Al Mutakabbiru*
    The Majestic
11. *Al Khaliqu*
    The Creator
12. *Al Baariu*
    The Evolver
13. *Al Musawwiru*
    The Fashioner
14. *Al Ghaffaru*
    The Forgiver
15. *Al Qahharu*
    The Subduer
16. *Al Wahhabu*
    The Bestower
17. *Ar Razzaqu*
    The Provider
18. *Al Fattahu*
    The Opener
19. *Al `Alimu*
    The All-Knowing
20. *Al Qaabidhu*
    The Constrictor
21. *Al Baasitu*
    The Expander
22. *Al Khaafidhu*
    The Abaser
23. *Ar Raafi`u*
    The Exalter
24. *Al Mu`izzu*
    The Honorer
25. *Al Mudhillu*
    The Dishonorer
26. *As Sami`u*
    The All-Hearing
27. *Al Basiru*
    The All Seeing
28. *Al Hakamu*
    The Judge
29. *Al `Adlu*
    The Just
30. *Al Latifu*
    The Subtle One
31. *Al Khabiru*
    The Aware
32. *Al Halimu*
    The Forbearing One
33. *Al-`Azimu*
    The Great One
34. *Al Ghafuru*
    The All-Forgiving
35. *As Shhakuru*
    The Appreciative
36. *Al `Aliyyu*
    The Most High
37. *Al Kabiru*
    The Most Great
38. *Al Hafizu*
    The Preserver
39. *Al Muqitu*
    The Maintainer
40. *Al Hasibu*
    The Reckoner
41. *Al Jalilu*
    The Sublime One

42. *Al Karimu*
   The Generous One
43. *Ar Raqibu*
   The Watchful
44. *Al Mujibu*
   The Responsive
45. *Al Waasi`u*
   The All-Embracing
46. *Al Hakimu*
   The Wise
47. *Al Wadudu*
   The Loving
48. *Al Majidu*
   The Most Glorious One
49. *Al Baa`ithu*
   The Resurrector
50. *As Shhahidu*
   The Witness
51. *Al Haqqu*
   The Truth
52. *Al Wakilu*
   The Trustee
53. *Al Qawwiyyu*
   The Most Strong
54. *Al Matinu*
   The Firm One
55. *Al Waliyyu*
   The Protecting Friend
56. *Al Hamidu*
   The Praiseworthy
57. *Al Muhsiyu*
   The Reckoner
58. *Al Mubdiu*
   The Originator
59. *Al Mu`idu*
   The Restorer
60. *Al Muhyiyu*
   The Giver of Life
61. *Al Mumitu*
   The Creator of Death

62. *Al Hayyu*
   The Alive
63. *Al Qayyumu*
   The Self-Subsisting
64. *Al Waajidu*
   The Finder
65. *Al Maajidu*
   The Glorious
66. *Al Waahidu*
   The Unique
67. *Al Ahadu*
   The Only One
68. *As Samadu*
   The Eternal
69. *Al Qaadiru*
   The Able
70. *Al Muqtadiru*
   The Powerful
71. *Al Muqaddimu*
   The Expediter
72. *Al Muakkhiru*
   The Delayer
73-74. *Al Awwalul Aakhiru*
   The First, The Last
75. *Az Zaahiru*
   The Manifest
76. *Al Baatinu*
   The Hidden
77. *Al Waali*
   The Governor
78. *Al Muta`ali*
   The Most Exalted
79. *Al Barru*
   The Source of All—Goodness
80. *At Tawwabu*
   The Acceptor of Repentance
81. *Al Muntaqimu*
   The Avenger
82. *Al `Afuwwu*
   The Pardoner

83. *Ar Raufu*
    The Compassionate
84. *Maaliku al-Mulku*
    The Eternal Owner of Sovereignty
85. *Dhu al-Jalaali wa al-Ikraam*
    The Lord of Majesty and Bounty
86. *Al Muqsitu*
    The Equitable
87. *Al Jaami`u*
    The Gatherer
88. *Al Ghaniyyu*
    The Self-Sufficient
89. *Al Mughniyyu*
    The Enricher
90. *Al Maani`u*
    The Preventer
91. *Ad Dhaarru*
    The Distresser
92. *An Naafi`u*
    The Creator of Good
93. *An Nuru*
    The Light
94. *Al Haadi*
    The Guide
95. *Al Badi`u*
    The Originator
96. *Al Baaqi*
    The Everlasting
97. *Al Waarithu*
    The Supreme Inheritor
98. *Ar Rashidu*
    The Guide to the Right Path
99. *As Saburu*
    The Patient

1. Ar Rahmanu, The All-Merciful:

Allah's Mercy encompasses everything. In this attribute, He is Beneficent and Merciful to all, believers as well as non-believers. He declares Himself in the Qur'an that His Mercy encompasses everything.[39] In one *hadith al-Qudsi*[40], Allah declares that His Mercy overtakes His Wrath. The very first verse in the Qur'an begins with this attribute. It reads: *"I begin in the name of Allah the All-Merciful, the Compassionate"* [41]

The understanding of this attribute in Islam, is that the all-Merciful Allah bestows His Mercy and love to all, believers as well as non-believers[42] The absolute uniqueness of this attribute of Allah is also that this word is the intensive form of the Arabic verb *R-H-M.* When a verb in this form in the Arabic language, is conjugated to become *Ra-H-Man*, it means intensely Merciful, intensely Compassionate. What makes this attribute even more interesting is the Arabic grammar use of the article *"al"*. In Islam, Allah's attribute is prefixed with this article. This makes all attributes of Allah, in any grammatically conjugated form, most intensifying to the extent that it cannot be compared with any other beings or things, or times or places. Allah does not depend on anything. *Ar-Rahman,* in its grammatically conjugated form, becomes an intensive form of All Merciful. With the article Al prefixed to the attribute, it now means that Allah is intensely, infinitely, all Merciful to all His creatures. His Blessings can never be totaled. He tells us in the Qur'an:

> Say: "If oceans were ink (wherewith to write out) the words of my Sustainer, sooner would the ocean be exhausted than the words of my Sustainer, even if we added another ocean like it, for its aid." (Qur'an, Ch.18:109).

At another place in the Qur'an, He reveals:

> And if all the trees on earth were pens and the ocean (were ink), with Seven oceans behind it to add to its (supply), yet would not the Words of Allah be exhausted (in the writing): for Allah is Exalted in power, full of Wisdom. (Qur'an, Ch. 31:27).

He creates, He nurtures, He provides, He protects, He preserves, He guides His creatures and leads them to the higher things of this life. In a beautiful passage in the Qur'an, Allah confirms:

> *Glorify the name of the Guardian-Lord, Most High, who has created, and further, given order and proportion; who has ordained laws and granted guidance. (Qur'an, Ch.87:1-3).*

Yet in one *Hadith al-Qudsi* Allah has revealed that He has divided all His Mercies and Blessings into one hundred parts. And all the Mercies and Blessings we live with and enjoy in this world is only one part from the hundred parts. The other Ninety-nine parts He has reserved for those who will enter His Paradise after the Day of Judgment.

2. *Ar Rahimu,* The Beneficent:
While Allah's Mercy encompasses everything as He says Himself in the Qur'an: *wa rahmatii wasi`at kulli shay'in* (My Mercy encompasses everything), it is for those who use these Bounties of Allah for the good causes, and according to His Will, that are rewarded with eternal rewards. For such people, He reveals: . . . *wa kaana bi al mu'minina Rahima (He is Rahim, Compassionate to (those who are) the believers).*[43] The reward for the believers, then, is not only that Allah is *Ar Rahman* to the believers but also that because believers use this Bounty of Allah according to the Will of Allah. Believers are known to Allah and are rewarded with the honor of the special reward meant exclusively for the righteous[44]. This bounteous reward reserved exclusively for the righteous shows Allah's attribute of *Rahimiyya* as shown in the verse cited above. This means that while the quality of *Ar Rahman* assures sustenance for everything and everybody in this world, believers as well as non-believers, tyrants as well as the good, just as well as unjust, it is different in the Hereafter. There, in the Hereafter, those who are salved are also blessed with Allah's special attribute of *Ar Rahimu* bestowed upon them. So, while the attribute of *Ar Rahman* assures the sustenance in this world, it is Allah's attribute of *Ar Rahimu,* that is the salvation of the Hereafter, reserved for the righteous.

3. *Al Maliku,* The Sovereign Lord:
There is no everlasting, true Sovereign of the heavens and the earth, what is in them and between them except Allah. Allah is the only real sovereign Lord. Real sovereignty means unending rule and power over everything celestial and terrestrial; and full power over life of everything celestial and terrestrial. Worldly rulers have their authority and power over a certain area, limited only to their territory, and that too, over only material things. Allah's Kingdom is not limited to only one small, specific territory.

He is the Ruler of the whole universe and *lahu ma fi as Samawaati wa ma fi alArdi* (whatever is in heavens and earth belongs to Him), for He is the One who created everything *ex-nihillo* and it belongs to Him alone. Further, everything that He has created, has a limited life cycle and does not endure forever. Allah Himself is the only One who does not die and He alone is the One who will remain forever. In the Qur'an we read:

> 'Say: "O God! Lord of Power (and Rule) You give power to whom you please, and You strip off power from whom you please: You endue with honor whom You please, and You bring low whom You please: in Your hand is all Good. Verily, over all things You have power. You cause the Night to gain on the Day, and You cause the Day to gain on the Night; You bring the Living out of the Dead, and You bring the Dead out of the Living; and You give the sustenance to whom You please, without measure.*[46]*

4. Al Quddusu, The Holy:

Allah's purity is unique. He is totally pure and uncorrupt in all His sovereignty, His names, His attributes, His essence, His words, His names and in everything else. He is devoid of any blemish in everything, including His Justice. In the Qur'an, we read:

> "God is He, than whom there is no other god—the Sovereign, the Holy One, the Source of Peace (and Perfection), the Guardian of Faith, the Preserver of Safety, the Exalted in Might, the Irresistible, the Supreme: Glory to God! (High is He) above the partners they attribute to Him).*[47]*

5. As Salaamu, The Source of Peace:

Allah is the Source of Peace. It emanates from Him, it is from Him and returns to Him. He will reward the believers with Salam (Peace) in Paradise. He reveals in the Qur'an:

Peace! a Word (of salutation) from the Sustainer, the Merciful.[48]

6. Al Mu'minu, The Guardian of Faith:

Allah is the One who illuminates the light of faith in the hearts of believers. He protects the one who takes refuge in Him. This is surely the Gift from Allah. It is the security that protects from the evil.[49]

7. Al Muhayminu, The Protector:

Allah is the Guardian and the Protector. He is the one who sees to the complete evolution in everything that He has created. Nothing, not even an iota of anything escapes His attention. It is He who watches all our deeds and rewards them fully.[50]

8. Al `Azizu, The Mighty:

Allah is the Almighty. No power or strength in the universe can stand against the Might of Allah. But in spite of Him being Almighty and total victorious over everything, Allah is not vengeful and does not destroy. He sees everything and has a record of every-thing of His slaves, but He does not destroy His opponents. In His total Mercy, He delays the punishment giving time and chance to His slaves to relent and remedy themselves. He is not vengeful in spite of Him being the Almighty. Allah's Kingdom is not corrupt in spite of the fact that He is the Almighty with absolute authority over everything. The Qur'an reveals a supplication Abraham makes to Lord the God Allah, in these words:

> "Our Lord! Send amongst them a Messenger of their own, who
> shall rehearse Your Signs to them and instruct them in Scripture
> and Wisdom, and sanctify them: For You are the Exalted in
> Might, the Wise.[51]

9. Al Jabbaru, The Compeller:

Allah is the One who completes the equation. He completes what lacks and enforces His Will without any opposition. Allah is the only One who brings ease to every difficulty. It is He who provides the means for the equation to be complete; Imam `Ali, the first Shi`a Imam and early rightly-guided Caliph used to supplicate: *Ya Jaabbiraa kulla kasirin wa Ya musahilla kulla `asirin* (O the Compeller! (you are the only one) who puts together all that is broken and You are (the only one) who brings ease to every difficulty. [52]

10. Al Mutakabbiru, The Majestic:

Allah is the only One to whom this attribute fits most perfectly. He is the only one who is truly the greatest. The others of His creation may think of themselves as great but that is just illusory because it is temporary and is bestowed only by Allah. Therefore, they do not have any right to assume this attribute, because this attribute, in actual fact, belongs only to Allah. Any claim from any of His other creation demonstrates only the arrogance and leads one to total astray. The very first to show this type of arrogance was the *Shaytaan* (Satan), the *Iblis*. It is for this reason that he is the *Shaytaan*, far from the guidance.[53] Any who follows the footsteps of *Shaytaan* by thinking himself or herself to be the greatest because of their temporary power, or fame or position or knowledge become of the company of the Shaytaan and are totally alluded from the fact that all power, prestige, fame or whatever else that makes them think great has been bestowed to them by Allah. It is only momentary, just as life itself is only momentary and is eaten up by the passing time. The only true greatness that is eternal and totally enduring forever is that of Allah's. So we see in the history, and indeed in our own lifetime, the end of many arrogant tyrants. All pride and arrogance was only temporary. Regardless, though, all are destined one day to die, and returned to the dust. The earth levels us all. The only true greatness is the Greatness of Allah Himself. He is *al Mutakabbiru*.[54]

11. Al Khaliqu, The Creator:

Allah is the Sole Creator of everything in its origin. He creates *ex nihillo from* nothing to something. He creates in proportion and gives it the power to obtain its sustenance. They are created with their instincts, pre-loaded. Allah reveals in the Qur'an:

> *"Glorify the name of thy Guardian—Lord, Most High, who has created and further, given order and proportion, who has ordained laws and granted guidance . . ."*[55]

His Will is enforced in everything He creates. Moreover, He states that He has created nothing in vain. Everything has been created with purpose. In His creation, there are no mythological accounts. You find in the creation of heavens and the planets perfect symmetry. It is the cosmos, not chaotic in the least. With no chaos, everything runs ever so smoothly. There is beneficence and mercy in it for the whole of the universe. The universe is amazing. The sustenance for humankind and all other creatures comes down from the heavens in the form of rains. Water mixes with the earth and things begin to grow with the warmth provided, again from the heavens, by the Sun glowing in the sky. The Qur'an reveals:

> *Behold! In the creation of the heavens and the earth; in the alternation of the Night and Day; in the sailing of the ships through the ocean for profit of mankind; in the rain which Allah sends down from the skies, and the life which He gives therewith to an earth that is dead; in the beasts of all kinds that*

> *He scatters through the earth; in the change of winds, and the clouds which they trail like their slaves between the sky and the earth; (here) indeed are Signs for a people that are wise.* [56]

12. Al Baariu, The Evolver :

Allah is the one who not only creates as we saw above, but He is the one who creates with harmony within itself, so that the thing created has a capacity to grow. There is a harmony working like a symphony within itself, where each thing is connected with the other, and while each has its own purpose, each is also connected with the other. Each works harmoniously with the other, in a perfect symphony, like the spokes of a wheel, like the parts of a clock. And each creation has a life-cycle of its own, pre-determined by Allah. It continues to grow and fulfill its purpose for which it was created.[57]

13. Al Musawwiru, The Fashioner:

Allah is the Originator, the Creator of all things. He shapes without using any model, and shapes in the perfect shape. Allah reveals this Attribute in many places in the Qur'an. Take this, for example. In the Qur'an we read:

> *"He has created the heavens and the earth in just proportions and has given you shape, and made your shapes beautiful and to Him is the final Goal.* [58]

Also, the Qur'an reveals that for Allah,

> *". . . when He intends a thing, His Command is Kun! (Be!) and it is! So Glory be to Him in whose hands is the dominion of all things: and to Him will you be all brought back).*[59]

14. Al Ghaffaru, The Forgiver:

It is only Allah who forgives. There is no other deity, or any saint who has the power or permission given by Allah to forgive for the sins one may commit against Allah. When we do something wrong to someone, of course we ask for that person's forgiveness before asking forgiveness from Allah. The human rights in Islam demands we ask forgiveness of the one we have harmed before turning to Allah for His forgiveness. Still, the ultimate forgiver of our sins is Allah. Similarly, we ask Allah for any sins committed directly against the injunctions of Allah. In both cases, the ultimate forgiver is only Allah.

"But, without doubt, I am (also) He that forgives again and again, to those who repent, believe, and do right—who, in fine, are ready to receive true guidance".[60]

15. *Al Qahharu*, The Subduer:

Allah is the Irresistible, the Ever-Dominating one. Nothing in the whole universe escapes Allah. While Allah *is al-Latifu*, (the Subtle, the One who loves with His delicate loving finesse), He is also *al-Qahharu*, the One who subdues the dark forces of tyranny, the arrogance, hypocrisy etc., In the complete story of Nabi Yusuf (Joseph) in the Qur'an, Nabi Yusuf is guiding the two prisoners he meets in the prison and advises them to worship only One God, Allah. Joseph asks them,

". . . Are many lords differing among themselves better, or the One God, Supreme and Irresistible? If not Him you worship nothing but names which you have named—you and your fathers—for which Allah has sent down no authority: the command is for none but Allah; He has commanded that you worship none but Him: that is the right religion, but most men do not understand." [61].

16. *Al Wahhabu*, The Grantor, The Bestower :

Allah is the Only true Bestower of everything in the universe. He bestows without condition and without asking for anything in return. Whether it is enriching the poor, or healing the sick, or giving the children to the barren. It is Only He who is the true Bestower, the *al-Wahhabu*. Allah creates means for His slaves on this earth through which He bestows. The Qur'an asks the believers in many verses, to thank Allah for creating the means through which He bestows. In the Qur'an, we read this supplication:

"O our Lord! Let not our hearts deviate now after You have guided us but grant us mercy from Your Own Presence; for You are the Grantor of bounties without measure".[62]

In another supplication reported to be from the fourth Shia Imam, Zayn al-Abidin, we read in reference to Allah being the grantor, as follows:

"Oh Allah! To You belongs the Praise, for it is You who created then proportioned, ordained and decreed, gave death and

granted life, made sick and healed, made well and afflicted, sat upon the Throne and encompassed the Kingdom.[63]

17. Ar Razzaqu, The Provider:

In the Islamic tradition, Allah is the true Sustainer par excellence. All sustenance comes only from Him. He is the Sustainer of the whole universe. And there is nothing in the Universe that He creates in vain. The vegetable kingdom receives its own sustenance from the heavens, in the form of rain and sunshine, which makes it grow to its fullest optimum. Likewise, everything else receives its own sustenance from Allah. The mineral kingdom receives its own sustenance and becomes useful to other creatures. The rainwater, as it falls from the heavens, mixes with the earth. Then it picks up several minerals as it flows in the form of a river rapidly from the mountains to the plains, providing sustenance to the earth and farmlands as it flows, now not so rapidly as when it was flowing through the mountains, now it is on the plains as all kinds of animals derive their sustenance from it. The Qur'an reveals that everything on the earth and the heavens Glorifies Allah. He reveals in the Quran that it is He, not the false deities, who is the Provider. All the bounties in the heavens and the earth have been created only by Allah. Nothing has been created in vain. Allah reveals this in the Qur'an:

> "To God belongs the dominions of the heavens and the earth; and God has power over all things. Behold! In the creation of the heavens and the earth, and the alteration of night and day—there are indeed Signs for men of understanding—men who celebrate the praises of God, standing, sitting, and lying down on their sides, and contemplate the (wonders of) creation in the heavens and the earth (with the thought) Rabbana maa khalaqta haadha batilan Our Lord the Sustainer! You have not created this universe in vain. Glory to You! Give us the salvation from the Penalty of the Fire. Our Lord! Any whom You admit to the Fire, truly You have covered with shame, and never will wrong-doers find any helpers. Our Lord! We have heard the call of one calling us to Faith (saying), 'Believe in the Lord' and we have believed. Our Lord! Forgive us our sins, blot out from us our iniquities, and take to Yourself our souls in the company of the righteous. Our Lord! Grant us what You promised to us through Your Messengers[65], and save us from shame on the Day of Judgment: for You never break your promise." [65]

18. Al Fattahu, The Opener:

Allah is the only True Opener of everything. He has the keys to the heavens and the earth. He is the True Solver of all problems and guides through all difficulties. His slaves therefore call just Him for their problems. It is He who provides the means for the problems to be solved. Of course He does not come down Himself but provides means either through inspiration for the problem to be solved or the means where a person in difficulty finds God-sent help. It is truly amazing how things work out in time. A slave of Allah recognizes and gives thanks to Allah for having removed his his difficulties by solving whatever that was needed to be solved. Allah opens up the way, even for those who are ungrateful to Allah. Allah's Mercy overtakes His wrath. Allah declares this in the Qur'an:

> "With Him are the keys of the Unseen, the treasures that none knows But He. He knows whatever there is on the earth and in the sea. Not(even) a leaf does fall but with His knowledge. There is not a grain in the darkness (or depths) of the earth, nor anything fresh or dry (green or withered),but is (inscribed) in a Record clear".[66]

19. Al `Alimu, The All-Knowing:

Allah is the Only One who truly knows it all. His knowledge is Absolute. No one can ever comprehend fully what Allah knows, except only as much as He wishes to bestow of His Knowledge. It is He, therefore, who grants the knowledge and wisdom to any-one, only in the proportion as much as He wishes. He reveals this Himself:

> "Allah, there is no god but He,—the Living, the Self-subsisting, Eternal. No slumber can seize Him nor sleep. To Him belongs whatever is in the heavens and whatever is in the earth. Who is it who can intercede with Him unless He permits? He knows what is ahead of them and what is behind them; and no one can comprehend His knowledge about anything except as He wishes. His Throne extends over the heavens and the earth; protection of both (the heavens and the earth) does not tire Him; and He is the Exalted, the Mighty".[67].

We find in the Qur'an example of Messengers and Prophets who were given special knowledge, but only as much as Allah Himself wanted. Thus in the Qur'an, Nabi Musa (Moses) is seen asking Allah for more knowledge. Allah guides Nabi Musa to a person (Nabi Khidhr who had even more knowledge bestowed upon Him by Allah). We also read in the Qur'an Allah asking *Rasul Allah*, (the Messenger of Allah) to supplicate with Allah for more knowledge: *O my Sustainer! Grant me Knowledge . . .* Therefore, in comparison to whatever knowledge we have, what we do not know is infinite. We do not know everything about the past, and we do not know anything about the future. But Allah knows it all:

"He is the First (of the firsts) and the Last (everlasting) The Evident and the Hidden: and He has full Knowledge of everything". (57:3).

20. Al Qaabidhu, The Constrictor:
Allah in His Wisdom alone knows what is best for His creatures. In His Hands is the Good and He has Power over all things. He moulds humankind through this life by several trials and tests. In doing so, He may constrict from anyone what He knows to be not good for them. He can do that also to test them if they truly are totally steadfast in only Him, in any state that He puts them through different kinds of natural disasters. It should also be perhaps noted that many a times mankind bring "bad times" upon themselves by their own doing. But if it is through natural causes, or causes that are totally beyond mankind's control, Muslims believe only Allah knows why He has put them through the trial. In His Mercy, though, even the trials are good because trials bring mankind more closer to Allah by accepting His Power and going through the *sabr*,(patience). The Qur'an reveals Allah does not put humankind to trials they can not bear. Although there is suffering during the times of constriction, a true believer remains steadfast to Allah knowing trials are from Him and thus moves even more closer to Allah submitting totally himself to the Will of Allah. Passing through the tests this way brings immense rewards. In the Islamic tradition, there are many sayings and proverbs regarding virtues of patience. One such saying reads: *Sabrun jamilun*, (patience, steadfastness is beautiful). It always brings about positive results.

21. Al Baasitu, The Expander:
Just as Allah is the Constrictor, He in His Mercy and Wisdom is also the Expander from all His Bounties. In this state as well, a true believer remains steadfast and does not exult or become arrogant and knows that everything that he has been give is from Allah. There again, he is going through the test and the trials, for He should know that in whatever He has been given, it is a trust from Allah. While in that state, he is comfortable, there are others who are less fortunate who have the right to receive help and assistance from the one who has more of Allah's bounty.

22. *Al Khaafidhu*, The Abaser:

Allah is the One who abases. Those in this world who are haughty and vainglorious because of their wealth and power, sometimes forget that whatever bounties they possess is actually what Allah has given them. They become arrogant thinking never will their wealth and power vanish. How foolish! Allah who has given the bounties can also take it away because He is also the Abaser. The cause of His abasing is always the human being himself. Allah does not like haughtiness and arrogance. *Allah* even in this Attribute is Merciful because per chance one would realize the wrongs one committed against himself when one had all the bounties. Allah gives time. The chances are that while he is still alive, he will repent and ask Allah's forgiveness for his sins and will find Allah's encompassing Mercy for He indeed is Forgiving, Merciful.

23. *I Ar Raafi`u*, The Exalter:

Allah is the Exalter. He abases the haughty and the arrogant (if they are lucky in this lifetime giving them chance to realize and repent), and He loves those who carry themselves in this life with being kind and compassionate towards others. Those who are giving, forgiving and forbearing always find a special Grace of Allah upon them. He exalts them by enlightening them in their hearts and in their status. In the final analysis, the real success is the success of the Hereafter. Whomever Allah exalts in the Hereafter is the one who has reached the final success. The Book of Allah calls this success the *fawz al-`azim* (The greatest Success). Believers in the Islamic tradition make this their daily prayer:

> *"O Allah! O our Lord the Sustainer! make us of these and grant
> us success both in this world and the Hereafter".*

24. *Al Mu`izzu*, The Honorer:

Allah is the Honorer. He Honors whom He wishes. The one who is honored by Allah has the special favors from Allah as he has been granted the *`izzah*, the dignity in the real sense of the word (as opposed to the *kibr,* the false pride one attributes to one owns self). Such a person goes through the life with special favor from Allah. Such a person is humble, kind and compassionate and he keeps himself away from anything that will displease Allah. That kind of person is looked up to as a person worthy of respect and honor by others as well. A person bestowed with such owner from Allah is not arrogant and if he errs, he repent to Allah for the mistakes he has committed and hoping that Allah will forgive him for Allah is often Forgiving, Merciful.

25. Al Mudhillu, The Dishonorer:
Just as Allah is the Honorer, He can also be the Dishonorer. This is indeed a sorry state, opposite the state of the one who has been honored by Allah. Such people live only for themselves and have made their earthly life the end of everything. Their earthly life, to them, is the final destination, the end of journey. Therefore, obtaining the maximum pleasure in this life is the goal, even if it is attained by means that are foul and unjust. There is no fear of the Hereafter. Their struggle in this life and all their energies are spent for the pursuit of the material world involving them in the major sin of *shirk*,[68] as they appear to be the worshippers of this world. The unfortunate result is that they begin to think and eventually begin to believe that what they have in this world is the result of their own struggles, that it is they who are the fashioners of their destinies. This thinking is discouraged in Islam because it may lead them to satanic ways, to the ways of the devil. Satan too, thought of himself great and was thrown out, disgraced by Allah for his pride and arrogance. That is the highest dishonor. Among prayers Muslims do one of the prayers asks Allah to always save them and protect them from such a catastrophe and from dishonor. Of these two Attributes, Allah reveals in the Qur'an:

> *Say: O Allah! The King of kings, You givest the power to whom You pleasest, and You strippest off power from whom You pleasest: You enduest with honor whom You pleasest, And You bringest low whom You pleasest: In Your Hand is all good. Verily, over all things You have Power.*[69].

26. As Sami`u, The All-Hearing:
Allah is the All-Hearing Sustainer of the universe. He hears everything in the universe, including our whispers, whether it passes through our lips or not, even our lurking thoughts. He hears the rustling of the leaves, the footsteps of even the smallest living creature. There is nothing that prevents any sound from reaching Allah. He hears all the sounds from one end of the earth to the other, whether it is in the night or the day, whether it is in the total wilderness, whether it is in the heavens or the earth. He hears all. Referring to believers calling Him in their supplications, Allah reveals:

> *When My servants ask you (O Muhammad) concerning Me, (tell them): I am indeed close (to them): I listen to the prayer*

*of every suppliant When he calls on Me: Let them also with a
will, listen to My call, and Believe in Me, that they may walk in
the right way.*[70]

27. *Al Basiru*, The All-Seeing:

Allah is the All-Seeing. He sees everything that we do. Just as He hears
everything and nothing escapes him from hearing everything, so does His
seeing everything in the universe. He has always been the All-Seeing, in
the past, the present and for all the future. On the Day of Resurrection,
human beings will be presented with full account of everything they did
because Allah has seen everything and everything is recorded. Everything
that we did on this earth will be presented to us and there will be no excuse.
To the human beings, Allah sees us although we cannot see Him. We can
see ourselves through the *Basirah*, a special intuition given to human
beings, who can see and understand themselves and know for sure that
although they cannot see Allah, He sees them. The Qur'an asks believers
to do good in their life through faith and good deeds. In Islam, faith alone
is not acceptable unless accompanied by good acts of compassion towards
others and never to think that God does not know about this. He reveals:

> *"And be steadfast in prayer and regular charity: and whatever
> good you send forth for your souls before you, you shall find it
> with Allah: for Allah sees well all that you do".*[71]

28. *Al Hakamu*, The Judge:

Allah is the One who orders. Allah is the One who is the True bringer
of Justice and Truth. The Final Judgment belongs only to Allah. When
Allah judges, nothing can oppose His Judgment for everything that is in
the heavens and the earth belongs only to Allah. He is the Just Judge. His
Mercy overcomes His wrath and His judgment prevails over everything.

29. *Al `Adlu*, The Just:

Allah's Justice is always fully equitable and Just. He may forgive whom He
wills and He may punish whom He wills, but this is only in the execution of
True justice. In this life on the earth, human beings cannot dispense with the
fullest justice. It is not possible for several reasons, the most important being
the limited life of a culprit. Take an example of a brutal tyrant who kills and
maims and destroys families. If he is captured and brought to justice, even
the maximum punishment cannot be the full justice for the crimes that this
tyrant might have committed. Also, he may be old and has lived the life
of his own. He may have other crimes in his record known only to Allah.

Fullest justice, fitting exactly to the crime, can be dispensed only with Allah. His Justice is opposite to tyranny, opposite to chaos. It is the fullest and true Justice. We should repent to Allah for any wrongs we might have committed or any actions that might have displeased Allah and ask for His Forgiveness and safety from committing any sins or acts displeasing to Allah. His Mercy overtakes His Wrath, and in that we all depend.

> *"Allah commands justice, the doing of good, and liberality to kith and kin, and He forbids all shameful deeds, and injustice and rebellion: He instructs you, that you may receive admonition".*[72]

30. *Al Latifu*, The Subtle One:

Allah is The Subtle, the One who knows and is the Creator and Fashioner of the finest and the most delicate. He is the One who is Himself the Finest, the Most Beautiful. The Finest of Himself are hidden in the secrets of the beauties of His Creations. In His Creation things fit beautifully into each other and become complementary. Truly, in His creation, everything in the earth and the heavens glorify Allah. He contains the minutest details that balance everything as they fit within each other: honey production in the bee, finest silk in the silk-worm, pearl within the oyster, fetus within the mother's womb. The Qur'an asks mankind to look at things around them and look within themselves and they will see the Divine handiwork of Allah. He is *Al Latifu*, the Finest, the Gentlest.

31. *Al Khabiru*, The Aware:

Allah is absolutely fully aware of everything, even the innermost thoughts. Everything that happens in the universe is known to Allah. He reveals in the Qur'an that even a falling leaf from a tree is known to Allah. He is aware of everything from the beginning to the end. He is aware of all things and all plans mankind makes, even those plans that are not yet actualized. Nothing escapes the attention of Allah. In more than one place in the Qur'an He reveals:

> *He knows what is in the heavens and on earth And He knows what you conceal and what you reveal Yes, Allah knows well the (secrets) of (all) hearts.*[73]

32. *Al Halimu*, The Forbearing One:

Allah is Forbearing. In His infinite Mercy, Allah gives respite. He gives time for His slaves to repent and to return to Him so that He can forgive.

In His Attributes, Allah's Mercy overtakes His Wrath. He loves to forgive more than to punish. Most in the mankind continue with their tyranny and corruption on this earth. If Allah were to take them to task as soon as they committed their crimes, none in the humankind would be left, but it is only the infinite Mercy of Allah the respite allows the fortunate ones to return to Allah repenting and mending their ways. Allah reveals:

> *But your Lord is Most Forgiving, full of Mercy. If He were to call them (at once) to account for what they have earned, then surely He would have hastened their Punishment: but they have their appointed time, beyond which they will find no refuge.*[74]

33. Al-`Azimu, The Great One:

Allah is not only the Sovereign, the Master, He is the Great. A worldly sovereign power has limitations over everything in his life. Indeed his life is controlled over everything. A worldly sovereign's power is not limitless. Also, he needs all the help from his ministers, from his footmen and has several departments working for him and the worldly sovereign power gets his authority only because Allah has willed it for him. It is not his own. But Allah is the Absolute Himself. He does not need any helper and nothing limits Allah. His is the Absolute authority. He is The Great One in every respect. Wherever we look, in the whole universe, we find the Signs of *Allah* witnessing His Greatness. He is the Grower, the Fashioner, the Ultimate Power, the All-Power. Nothing can compare the Greatness of Allah. Everything else in the heavens and the earth glorifies Allah.

34. Al Ghafuru, The All-Forgiving:

Allah is the All-Forgiving and hiding our faults from others, including angels. Allah in His Mercy, protects us from feeling ashamed on the day of Judgment by hiding our faults even from angels and in this world from humankind, if we sincerely turn towards Him seeking His forgiveness. Allah is also *al-Gaffar*. It means that He, in His absolute Mercy, protects us from suffering by even making us forget of our sins if we have turned towards Him asking for forgiveness most sincerely. Allah helps us become someone of resolve who does not repeat such sins.

35. As Shhakuru, The Appreciative:

Allah returns the good with multiplied good. He appreciates His slaves who do the good deeds prescribed by Allah and as demonstrated in the *Sunnah*.[75] A true slave of Allah is the one who recognizes that all he has is not really his; it is given to him by Allah. Such a person will not be blinded and go into abusing the bounties but will use the bounties of Allah recognizing his role as merely a steward of Allah on the earth. He will fully partake and thank Allah for the grace and bounties and will use the portion of it in the way of Allah helping the less unfortunate ones and helping in the cause of Allah. The bounties need not only be wealth. Muslims believe every part of their body is a gift from Allah. All their sensual perceptions, if used for the pleasure of *Allah* count as good deeds and because Allah is *As Shhakuru*, the Appreciative, He multiplies it. So, to a Muslim, spending in the way of Allah for the benefit of humankind increases wealth, it does not decrease, because Allah is Appreciative. The benefits of this are seen in this world but the real benefits of these, in multiplied form and eternal, will be for the Hereafter. This guarantee is given in so many places in the Qur'an that if one has faith and does good deeds, Allah will make him enter the Paradise in which he will dwell forever.

36. Al `Aliyyu, The Most High:
Allah is the only One who is truly the Highest. This does not mean highest in terms of height but in terms of His Attribute. He is the highest of the high in all His Attributes. He is as close to us as mankind's jugular vein. He is with them wherever they are. He listens to everything mankind utters. He is aware in His Attributes of even what is hidden in the depths of the earth or buried in the mountains. He is the highest in all His attributes, in all His qualities. He is above of the above, the Highest, He is *al-`Aliyyu*.

37. Al Kabiru, The Most Great:
Allah's Greatness can never be fathomed by the human mind because of its finite nature. As one scholar explains by saying that Allah's Greatness stretches from before the beginning until after the end. The greatness of all conceivable greatness from the beginning to the end is only His creation and proof of His Greatness. We use the term "infinite" in relation to the heavens and to time. This attribution of infinity to created things is only because of proper conception of them will not fit into our understanding. His Greatness, therefore, can never be comprehended by us, even though we, the human beings, are the best of His creation.

38. Al Hafizu, The Preserver:
Allah is The Preserver, the One who knows all that has already happened and all that is happening now and all that will happen. Everything that we think, and do, Allah is not only aware but he also preserves it and nothing is lost with Allah. But He is also The Protector. He protects all from harm.

He sent Prophets and Messengers to guide humankind and to protect us from the harm.

39. Al Muqitu, The Maintainer, The Nourisher:
Allah is the Maintainer. He creates the created and then the created is nourished and maintained throughout its life. He nourishes from the time of inception of His creation to the death of the created. Every body's nourishment is guaranteed. Allah does not abandon His creatures after they have been created by Him. We find in all His beautiful names that He is *al-Khaliqu, al-Baari'u, al-Musawwiru, al-Fattaahu* and all the other *Asmaa`*(Names) of Allah in which He is the King, who is the First, the Last, the Final Judge for those who took away the rights of others denying them what lawfully belonged to them.

40. Al Hasibu, The Reckoner:
Allah is The Reckoner. That is to say, that He is the One who takes the account of everything that mankind does. The *Kiram al-Katibin*, the two angels, who sit on the shoulders of all human beings, make note of everything that they do. The book of deeds will be presented to all in which will be written everything as Allah revealed in the Qur'an. Humankind will say when presented with that book on the Day of Accounting: What kind of Book is this? There is nothing small or big that is not recorded in this. Human being's life on this earth is controlled by time, the greatest capital. To a monotheist, how humankind spend their time on this earth is very important, because every second that passes will not return. It brings humankind closer to their final Day of Accounting. Then it will be determined, after women and men have given the account of their life on this earth, as to what kind of eternal life Hereafter they will be put into. The successful life is the life in the Paradise. To achieve that success, how did one spend the time on this earth will be the biggest factor in accounting.

41. Al Jalilu, The Mighty One:
Allah is the Sustainer of Majesty, of Might. Allah's Might, His Majesty can not be measured with any other might or energy. There is no resemblance because Allah's Energy, Allah's Might or His Essence can never be measured into any measure, whether that measure is of time, or space. Allah's Might is everywhere, in everything. He is the Creator of everything. All the knowledge is His. All the Power is His alone and it is He who encompasses all the universe, everything that is in it and everything that is between it. Just as He is Great, His Mercy is also great. His Generosity is great. His Treasures are inexhaustible. Allah is the Source and the Owner of all the Greatness, or the Goodness, all the Generosity, all the Mercy, all the Beneficence, all the Compassion, all the Perfection. He is the goal of all the hopes. He is the True Might, the Mighty, the Sublime.

42. Al Karimu, The Generous One:
Allah in His infinite Mercy, is The Most Generous One. He displays His Mercy upon the sinners when He could punish them. He gives respite and allows time to repent. He forgives when He could punish. He gives all kinds of chances and opportunities for His slaves to turn to Him. Allah keeps all His promises. He has promised in the Qur'an and through the a*hadith* from His Messenger, *Rasul Allah* (the Messenger of Allah) that His Mercy overtakes His Wrath. He promises in the Qur'an that all the good deeds His slaves do are multiplied by ten times where as any bad deed is counted just the once. He is Generous and gives refuge even to those who have been ungrateful. In His generosity over humankind, He gave them special faculties as He raised their status to make them His vicegerents on this earth. He has truly raised the status of the children of Adam and made them of the best creation. And in His generosity over those who submitted to Him and became His *Ummah.,* Muslims believe He made them the best of His creation and gave them the opportunity to enjoin the good and forbid evil. This gift is the generosity itself.

43. Ar Raqibu, The Watchful:
Allah is Ar Raqibu, that is to say, He watches everything and everything is known to Him. A believer, who has reached the stage of the highest faith, the *Ihsaan,* will be acutely aware of this fact, always, that although he may not see Allah but Allah watches him, always. Such a person will not be heedless and will go through this life with the *Taqwa* (God-Consciousness) of Allah in all his attitude. Such a person does not need recognition from the world of any good deed that he does for surely his actions would be

to attain the pleasure of Allah. He knows for sure that the world may not recognize or reward him for his good deeds but Allah recognizes each and every good deed and in His Promise in the Qur'an each good deed is multiplied by ten times. It does not mean that such a person is infallible. Far from it!. Such a person will make mistakes but his being conscious that Allah has watched all his deeds, he will be conscious in repenting to Allah beseeching His Help and his Mercy. And surely, as we have already seen in other (Names) of Allah, His Mercy overtakes His Wrath. What such a person will always be watchful of would be the desires of his own *Nafs*, (conscious self) of the carnal desires. Muslims believe that the true enemy of humankind on the earth to watch, are the *Shayatin* (Satans) of this world.

44. *Al Mujibu*, The Responsive:

Allah responds to His creatures. As already explained above, He is closer to even mankind's jugular veins. Allah knows their needs before even they realize them and He fulfills their needs and also their wants. What Allah wants from them, in Islamic belief, is the definite belief and trust in Him. They must know for certain that Allah hears their supplications to Him and He will fulfill their wants. In His mercy, He knows when it will be best to give what we ask. He asks for their belief in Him as the condition in the Qur'an:

> *When My servants ask you concerning Me, I am indeed close (to them): I listen to the prayer of every suppliant when he calls on Me: Let them also, with a will, listen to My call, and believe in Me: That they may walk in the right way.* (Qur'an, 2:186).

When humankind responds to the injunctions of Allah it is the manifestation of the attribute of being *Mujib* (responsive). Muslims believe it is the Grace of Allah upon humankind that He gives humankind the opportunity to be responsive to the Command s of Allah and to give to others through their hands.

45. *Al Waasi`u*, The All-Embracing:

Allah's vastness is limitless. There is no limit in any of His attributes. No one can ever find and say "here is the limit". In all of His attributes and indeed in His *Dhaat* Allah is Vast. His vastness is seen in His creation. Not only He is vast, Allah is faultless. There is no fault in His creation. Just as He is endless in every way, all His attributes, He is also endless in His tolerance towards human beings. The wrongs of humankind on this earth could be punished immediately if Allah so wished, but in His vastness and in His attributes of being Beneficent and Merciful, He gives respite but also never fails in His Promise for retributions to the doers of evil and multiplied Rewards to the doers of good. Allah's vastness is reflected in His best creation, the human being, the children of Adam. It is from humankind that Allah selected His Prophets and His Messengers and it is from the human beings that He selected and chose *Rasul Allah*, the Messenger of Allah, as the epitome of mercy to the universe. It is through Him being *al-Waasi`u* that He ennobled human beings. He reveals in the Qur'an:

> *And We have certainly honored the children of Adam; provided them with transport on land and sea, given them for sustenance things good and pure; and conferred on them special favors, above a great part of Our creation.* (Qur'an, Ch.17:70)

46. *Al Hakimu*, The Wise:

Allah is the One who is The Wise; as He is the One who possesses the perfect and the most sublime knowledge. In Allah's knowledge, there is no uncertainty and there is no doubt. His Knowledge is everlasting. Its extinction is not conceivable. But in His Knowledge, Allah also has fullest mastery and fullest command over all the finer points. This claim only applies to Allah. Everything has been created by Allah and there is full wisdom in Allah's creation. In His Wisdom, in everything that He has made lawful, there are enormous benefits for humankind, there is progress and there is success for both in this life and or the believers, in the life Hereafter. In the things that He has forbidden, there is no good for humankind. Struggling for those kind of pursuits leads to eventual destruction because there is no wisdom in it.

47. *Al Wadudu*, The Loving:

Allah desires only all good for his best creation, a creation in whom He blessed with His own Spirit, the humankind. So Allah is *Ar-Rahman*, the All-Merciful, and the object of all His Mercy is upon His creation, the best of the creation of which is the human being, whom He honored and made him the object to which even the angels were asked to prostrate because man carries in him the Spirit, which Allah Himself breathed in him. So, the attribute *Al-Wadudu* of Allah upon humankind is the manifestation of Allah being the all-Merciful, the all-compassionate and wishing for the humankind success and honor. It is in His infinite love, totally unconditional, upon His servants that has given them the ability to pursue and achieve whatever they want in this life. He has given them the ability to understand and receive the Truth. It is through His being the Loving Allah that He gave them the ability to choose between the right and the wrong, between the Truth and the Falsehood. His attribute of being *Ar Rahman* is for all while they are on this earth. Muslims relate to one tradition from the Prophet Muhammad where he is reported to have said the love of Allah for humankind exceeds the love a mother has for her child. Man may choose to accept the love of Allah and become grateful and manifest that by himself being the `*Abd al-Wadudu* (the slave of the Loving Allah) in his life towards others, or they may become ungrateful and disbelievers. Allah in His Mercy is The Loving Being.

48. *Al Majidu*, The Most Glorious One:

Allah is the most Glorious One, He is the most Majestic, He is the most Honored One. He is the most Powerful. No power can reach Him or subdue Him. But He is the closest to His servants, closer even as explained with other attributes, than their own jugular vein. *Huwa kuntum ayna maa kuntum*, He is with you wherever you are, He tells humankind in the Qur'an. His bounties are immense, they are infinite. He loves His servants and has mercy upon them. So the scholars have explained in this attribute of Allah an element of His Majesty, His Power, His Glory. The other is His Honor, as seen clearly in all His creation, in His actions. He is the one who is truly praised for His Attribute of being *al-Majidu*. Those of His servants recognizing this and seeking only His ultimate pleasure in all their actions, find that they receive enormous strength and honor for themselves. Muslim exegetes tell us that all have to be Allah's `*Abd,* the slaves of *al-Majidu,* the slaves of *Allah* the most Majestic, the most Glorious.

49. *Al Baa`ithu*, The Resurrector:

Islamic tradition tells us that Allah has promised to all people in all nations through all the Prophets that He will resurrect the humankind from the dead and give life back to them on the Day of Resurrection. That Day will be the Day of Resurrection. He will raise humankind from the death and will bring out all their actions and all theirr deeds and even everything that they thought of during their lifetime on the earth. In the Chapter of The Cave, in the Qur'an, *Surat al-Kahf* Allah reveals:

> *And the Book (of deeds) will be placed (before you) and you will see the sinful in great terror because of what is (recorded) Therein; they will say, "Ah! Woe to us! What a book is this! It leaves out nothing small or great, but takes account thereof!"*

They will find all that they did, placed before them: and not (even) one will your Sustainer treat with (any) injustice." [76].

The exegetes tell us that this attribute of Allah can bring about revolution in one's life to the progress both in this world an in the Hereafter, because understanding of this makes a person tread through this life with honesty and due diligence. A God-fearing person will not harm others through this life and will be compassionate and kind towards others. On the other hand, those who think that the only real end of human being's life is death, will be at a great loss because it is not that they did not hear the truth of the Hereafter from their own faiths. There is no faith that does not have a belief in the Hereafter and that the Hereafter is based on our deeds on this earth (in polytheistic faiths, the afterlife is based on *Karma,* it still deals with the deeds). Death from the earthly life, therefore, is not going away into oblivion. Rather, it is the true reality that death from earthly life is only a transfer to the other phase of life, the *Barzakh,* (purgatory) where the phase will remain to the Day of Resurrection. The reality of the afterlife is mentioned in several places in the Qur'an. Some examples are:

Chapter 30:40, *"It is Allah who has created you: further, He has provided for your sustenance; then He will cause you to die; and again He will give you life. Are there any of your (false) 'partners' who can do any single of these things? Glory to Him! And High is He above the partners they attribute (to Him).*

Chapter 20:55, *"From the (earth) We created you, and into it We shall return you, and from it We shall bring you out once again".*

Chapter 22:7, *"And verily The Hour will come: there can be no doubt about it, or about (the fact) that Allah will raise up all who are in the graves".*

50. *As Shhahidu,* The Witness:
Allah is the Witness to each and every thing. There is nothing that is ever hidden from Allah. He is the knower of both the visible and the invisible. He is witness even to the lurking thoughts in our minds. Whether the thing is hidden in the mountains or beneath the earth, In the heavens, in the space or anywhere, Allah is aware of it and is a witness to it. Allah tells us in the Qur'an that when we plan anything in secret, we are never alone. Allah is the witness to that as well. He is Omnipresent, Omniscient. He is the Evident, the hidden. Nothing escapes Him and all that we do will be shown to us in full detail just as we saw in His Attribute of being *al-Ba`ithu.*

51. *Al Haqqu*, The Truth:

Allah is The Truth. The ultimate Truth is that whose essence is valid in itself and is the cause and is necessary for all other existence. That is Allah. His existence is not dependent on something else but all other things are dependent on Him. This makes everything else temporal and makes Him the Eternal. It is existent by itself and is not influenced by any other. Everything else that requires existence take their existence from Him. They are changing; and as soon as they come to existence, they are affected by their life-cycle given to them by virtue of creation by Allah. This means that their existence is temporal and under control of Allah who has given them the life-cycle of their own. Under this life-cycle their existence is time-bound and temporal. When their life-cycle is up, they disappear and what appeared to be truly existing at one time is no more. The true existence is only of Allah the Eternal, the everlasting, the Truth.

52. *Al Wakilu*, The Trustee:

Allah is the ultimate and the only True Trustee. Allah is not deficient, not even an iota, in everything and leaves nothing deficient or undone. He does everything but He does not need anything to be done for Him. Likewise, Allah replaces anything He wants in the heavens and the earth. But nothing can replace Him. He is the Eternal, the Everlasting, the Compassionate, the Merciful. He is the ultimate Trustee. Placing trust in Him is to believe in all of His attributes as the most complete without any deficiency. Trust in Him, therefore, is the most satisfying thing. There is no one else in the whole universe who can do better than He does. This is the *Tawakkal* in Allah. Total trust in Allah. This is the greatest resource for His creatures. It is the greatest treasure. This requires, at the same time, effort form His servants. Muslim exegetes tell us that we cannot just sit and hope for things to happen. That would not be *Tawakkal*. Trust in Allah means endeavors from us with the full conviction that the result is in the Hands of Allah. For in His Hands is all good and He is the One who makes things happen and bring them to fruition. We have to endeavor and pray to Allah with fullest conviction that He is the ultimate Trustee. We can trust anything to Him to fulfill for us.

He asks us to ask from Him and He does not turn us away. Trust in Him that He listens everything and that in His Hands is the fullest authority over everything. He will fulfill it completely without leaving anything deficient or undone. For He is the ultimate Trustee, *Al-Wakil*.

53. *Al Qawwiyyu*, The Most Strong:

Allah is the one with complete power, with complete strength. Also, His strength, His power is unconditional. He does not need anyone's help but everyone needs His Help. There is nothing difficult for Allah. No one can ever subdue Him; but He can subdue all. His throne extends over the heavens and the earth. He is the Creator of the universe that includes from the most complex to even the smallest, one-cellular creature, the Amoeba. His Strength is infinite and none is above Allah. Allah's power is witnessed in everything around us. In the Qur'an, Allah points to Signs for humankind to reflect and ponder over them. In one comprehensive passage we read:

> *"Among His Signs is this, that He created you from dust, and then behold, you are men scattered (far and wide). And among His Signs is this, that He created for you spouses from among yourselves, that you may dwell in tranquility with them, and He has put love and mercy between your (hearts): verily in that are signs for those who reflect. And among His Signs is the creation of the Heavens and the Earth, and the variations in your languages and your colors: verily in that are signs for those who know. And among His Signs is the sleep that you take by night and by day, and the quest that you (make for your livelihood) out of His bounty: verily in that are signs for those who hearken. And among His Signs He shows you the lightning by way of both fear and hope, and He sends down rain from the sky and with it gives life to the Earth after it is dead; verily in that are signs for those who are wise. And among His Signs is this, that Heaven and Earth stand by His command: then when He calls you, by a single call, from the Earth, behold, you (straightaway)come forth. To Him belongs every being that is in the Heaven and on Earth; all are devoutly obedient to Him. It is He who begins (the process) of creation: then repeats it: and for Him it is most easy. To Him belongs the loftiest similitude in the Heavens and the Earth: for He is Exalted in Might, Full of Wisdom".*(Qur'an, Ch. 30:20-27).

54. Al Matinu, The Firm One:
Allah is Absolute in all His attributes. The attribute of *al-Matin* is the all-Pervasive firmness. No force can interfere with this firmness. No force can oppose it or create any hindrance in the firmness of Allah. He extends His Compassion and love to His servants and no one can oppose this or stop this from reaching His servants. There is no power in the heavens

or the earth that can prevent His Mercy reaching His servants. All the same, there is no power in the heavens and the earth that can prevent His Wrath reaching its target. Muslim supplications to Allah include plea to Him asking Allah to save them from His anger and wrath; and that He be pleased with them and favor them with His blessings, Amen. A true servant of Allah should always hope for Forgiveness and blessings from *Allah* and should always fear His punishment. All other fears disappear when that happens.

55. *Al Waliyyu*, The Protecting Friend:
Allah is, to the believers, the Protecting Friend. The Qur'an reveals:

> *Allah is the Protecting Friend of the believers He removes them
> from darkness to the Light . . .* (Qur'an, Ch. 2:257)

Allah's love in the hearts and minds of the believers is so great that in His remembrance they find tranquility in their hearts. They are not constrained. No fear or grief touches them because they have given themselves up to Allah. He keeps them safe from fear and grief. To give to the cause of Allah in Islam means to have full faith and go through this life with good deeds that requires Muslims to be kind and compassionate towards others. This includes almsgiving to less fortunate and to help others in need. He enlightens their hearts. The greatest honor through this life is to reach the status where Allah becomes the *wali* (friend) of a believer. At that point, they begin to see with Divine light as they take lessons and learn from everything they hear and see. They become the *awliya* (friends) of Allah and go through this life fulfilling their duties, seeking forgiveness from Allah for errors and mistakes they commit in executing their duties through this life. They hope and await the eternal blessing of the Hereafter as they go through this life. That is the highest expectation, the Supreme Success that all should strive for. In the Qur'an, Joseph is seen supplicating these words:

> *"O my Lord! You have indeed bestowed on me some power,
> and taught me something of the interpretation of dreams and
> events—O You creator of the heavens and the earth! You are my
> Protector in this world and the Hereafter. You take my soul (at
> death) as a Muslim (i.e. one submitting to Your Will), and unite
> me with the righteous.*(Qur'an, Ch. 20:101)

Believers in the Islamic faith have the ardent desire that Allah grant them the status of those who truly submitted their will to Allah during their lifetime.

56. Al Hamidu, The Praiseworthy:

Allah is the Most Praiseworthy. Muslims ask, "and why not?" Think about this. Is there any bounty that you can think of whose source is not Allah the Exalted? Then look at the form and the symmetry and the perfectness of the bounties from Allah. Look at yourself and the faculties that you have. A human being is like a mini-universe. In the creation of a human being and his faculties you find cosmos, not chaos. In his form, you find perfect symmetry. The faculties of hearing, seeing, smelling, tasting, touching, and how through the use of these faculties a human mind begins to process ideas to arrive at rational conclusions! Now look at the universe and you find cosmos. Look at the planets in the sky. Do you find chaos, or cosmos? It is certainly cosmos. Everything computed and runs its course. Night changing into day and day changing into night. So precisely computed that we can tell by seconds as to when the eclipses are going to occur. Look at how the weather cycle runs and how the seasons change. All this created by just the One Creator, Allah. He declares in the Qur'an:

> Say: "If the ocean were ink (wherewith to count in writing) the words (bounties) of my Sustainer, sooner the ocean would be exhausted than would the words of my Sustainer, even if we added another ocean like it, for its aid. [77]

And again, in Chapter we read:

> And if all the trees on earth were pens and the ocean (were ink) with (other) seven oceans behind it to add to its (supply) yet would not the Words of Allah be exhausted (in the writing): for Allah is exalted in power, full of Wisdom. [78]

Monotheists of all traditions think it would be unfortunate if one was to deny the bounties of the Beneficent, the Merciful Allah the God? Muslims claim that revelations in all monotheistic faiths show Allah is the One who is the true *Al-Hamidu*, the Praiseworthy.

57. Al Muhsiyu, The Absolute Reckoner:

Allah is the Absolute Reckoner. He is the Absolute Possessor of all the knowledge, including all the quantitative knowledge. Allah knows everything not only in its whole form but also knows all its components and how it is analytically separated. He knows all its parts, to the atom. He knows the number of units, what are they composed of and how many atoms they carry. There is nothing hidden from Allah. Nothing unknown to Him. He knows the number of leaves on trees and knows how many have dried up. He has the knowledge of even the fallen leaves from the tree. In a beautiful verse in the Qur'an, He reveals:

> *With Him are the keys of the unseen, the treasures that none Knows but He. He knows whatever there is on the earth and in the sea. Not a leaf does fall but with His knowledge : There is not a grain in The darkness (or depths) of the earth, nor anything fresh or dry, But is (inscribed) in a Record clear (to those who can read).* [79]

There is absolutely nothing hidden from Allah as we have already seen in the other attributes of Allah already described. He is *al `Alim,* the All-Knowing, He is *al-Basiru,* the All-Seeing, He is *as-Sami`u,* the All-Hearing and other attributes already described. And so, the record of all the deeds of mankind will be presented to them on the Day of Judgment when nothing will be hidden, the good that they did or the bad. And the good, even if it was as small as the mustard-seed will be accounted for and rewards given. And if the deed was even the smallest, as small as the mustard seed, it will be accounted for and retributions given accordingly, unless if Allah forgives. Thus Allah reveals:

> *On that Day will men proceed in companies sorted out to be shown the deeds that they (had done). Then shall anyone, who has done (even an) atom's weight of good, see it! And anyone who has done (even an) atom's weight of evil, shall see it.* [80]

58. Al Mubdiu, The Originator:

Allah is the Originator of each and everything, of all. He is the Creator of everything. He creates *ex-nihillo.* That is to say, He creates a thing without that thing having been created before. Allah does not need any specimen or sample or model or pattern to copy from. He creates from nothing into something that is so perfect and that has a guidance in it to pro create. Allah existed before anything was created by Him. Allah originated the creation to make His Beauty and His Perfection known; at the same time that His

Compassion, His Mercy should be known. He made the original creation and gave it the guidance to perpetuate itself by pro creating of its own specie in accordance with causes of the Divine Order, which also He created. Allah created humankind from nothing and gave them the sensual perceptions of touching, smelling, seeing, hearing and tasting and gave them the rational perceptions to process in their minds through the sensual perceptions. And created for each of His creation the time-cycle within which they grow and reach their maturity and return to Him in the end when He will restore them again on the Day of Resurrection. Can anybody else do that except Allah? Muslim exegetes ask how can anyone then worship anything else but Allah? They quote a famous verse from the Qur'an: *Inna lillahi wa inna ilayhi raaji'un,* Indeed we are from Allah and Unto Allah is our final return.

59. Al Mu'idu, The Restorer:
Allah is The Restorer. He originates His creation from nothing. He also is the Restorer. He gives life and at appointed time takes away life on the earth. Allah has also promised mankind that He will restore them on the Day of Resurrection, even after their bodies have become decomposed and reduced to dust in graves. While we are alive, through His will, we can use all our given faculties. Through this faculties, the wisest person would recognize the Truth that Allah is the One who has created us; that this life is designed and is not without any purpose; that this earth is a temporary sojourn; that this earth is only a testing ground and what we do on this earth is what is going to count. Then He will take the life away. This, humankind calls 'the death'. But in real terms, as Muslim theologians explain, death is not really the end of life. It is only a transfer to the phase they know as *Barzakh,* the purgatory. The end of life will only be after the Final Day of Resurrection. We see death happens to people every day. It is only a matter of time when this will also happen to us. But then also that Allah will restore this life for the accounting for Allah to judge how our life has been. The Promise that will be fulfilled for sure, as Allah will restore mankind and return life to them or this purpose.

60. Al Muhyiyu, The Giver of Life:
Allah is the one who gives life. It is the name that is derived from bringing into being. That is, from *ex-nihillo,* from nothing, to life. Allah brings into existence from nothing, so that it becomes life. Allah also ordains for a thing He brings into existence, a life-cycle of its own. So if existence is life, the act of bringing into existence is called *ihyaa.* The opposite of this, as we shall see in the next attribute of Allah is al-*Mumitu,* the Creator

of Death. This act of bringing death is called the *Imaata*. No one except Allah is the only one who created our life in our mother's womb and then nourished us and gave us all the sensual faculties of seeing, hearing, smelling, touching, tasting and hearing. It is also He alone who gave us the faculties of rational perception so that we can make choices in life. This is a special gift given to humankind. Man is the only being who can change the landscape. Animals do not. Man can plan, and then execute his plan. Animals go only by instinct, not by drawing plans. This ability to make choices is of utmost importance for our success in this life but most importantly for our Hereafter. Recognizing and realizing Allah and making the right choice of believing in Him and leading the life pleasing to Allah is the right choice. Muslims believe the choice not to believe in Him is a choice of destruction and a failed life in the world and also in the Hereafter.

61. *Al Mumitu*, The Creator of Death:

Allah is the Creator of death. As explained in the Attribute of *al-Muhyi* above, Allah is also the Creator of Death. This is ordained for all living things. All things must and will die. What makes a human being unique is that he carries within himself also the Spirit of Allah. This Spirit never dies. It is eternal. What will die is the body and its flesh, because it is temporal. When this happens, the Soul returns to where it came from in the first place. There is no death for our soul because it is the Spirit which Allah blew into humankind when He created him from the clay. It is the Spirit that gives him the rational quality to think in this life and allows him to make choices.

62. *Al Hayyu*, The Alive:

Allah is The Alive. He is the only Being who does not degenerate, depreciate or die. He is the Ever-Living. He is in His Attribute of *al-Hayyu* the one who acts and perceives things. All that is known and will be known is within the Knowledge of Allah. The quality being *al-Hayyu* means that with the exception of Him, everything else is held within the limits of its action and its realization. It is only under the full perception of *al-Hayyu* all the other objects of perceptions are moved. There is nothing in the heavens or the earth that is not under His action. Nothing escapes from *Allah* and as explained previously, everything else has a limited life within a particular time-span simply because the Attribute of being *al-Hayyu* (the Ever-Living) does not belong to them. It belongs only to Allah who is the Only One who is *al-Hayyu,* the Ever-living, the Eternal, the one not affected by time, for even time is created by Him and even time has a limited life-cycle of its own. The Only truly ever-alive is only Allah.

63. *Al Qayyumu,* The Self-Subsisting:

Allah is the one and only upon Him depends everything else in the heavens and the earth, what is in them and what is between them. Allah Himself is Self-existing. He depends on nothing but everything else depends upon Him. He is the Cause for the existence of everything else, and everything, except He is not eternal. The only Being that will remain Eternal and forever is Allah. We take an example of how everything is dependent on Allah: A human being, for example, is alive because of the soul within him. As long as the soul is within him, he continues to have life within him. All the cells of his body, everything, depends on the soul. But once the soul leaves the body, he dies. Nothing now will function. Similarly, the whole universe. Everything in the universe, the movement of planets, the changing of the day into night and night into day, the water-cycle, the growth of vegetation, the animal kingdom, the vegetable kingdom and the mineral kingdom, everything absolutely, depends on Allah. He is the Cause of each and every thing, Everything depends on Him but He depends on no one. He is the *al-Qayyumu,* the Self-Subsisting.

64. *Al Waajidu,* The Absolute Founder:

Allah is the Absolute Founder without any needs. Allah is neither in want for anything nor does He lack any thing. Allah does not need to find anything. Everything is in His presence at all times. He exercises His Will without having need for, or to find for any tools. Muslims believe God sees us and is with us all the times, wherever we are. It is He who has founded for us life and death in the age and time in the history of His choosing. When we need anything, we need not make any appointment with Allah. It is the Divine Mercy and Blessings of Allah that we turn at once to Allah for He is the Finder, the Provider, the Nourisher.

65. *Al Maajidu,* The Most Glorious:

Allah is the Most Glorious. This Attribute of Allah is the same as *al-Majidu* (previously described) except that this has greater extensiveness in meaning. Allah is infinitely generous. He gives to His slaves the gift of good character and endows them with the ability to do good works in their life time. Humankind should therefore pray to Allah so that they remain endowed with this Blessing. In His Mercy, He gives them the rewards for the good deeds they do (in spite of the fact that it is He who endows them

with this ability in the first place). Allah hides their weaknesses and their errors. It is He who relieves difficulties and is
Benevolent. He is the Most Glorious.

66. *Al Waahidu*, The Unique:

Allah is He who is Uniquely One. There is none other like Him. This uniqueness is expressed everywhere, in all the creation in the heavens and the earth. He cannot be divided and cannot be separated. So, if we take the example about all His attributes, we find that none of His attributes can be separated from each other. All His *Sifaat*, His attributes are One in His *Dhaat*, in his Essence, in Allah. He cannot be separated into component parts. Neither can He be duplicated. He is uniquely the One. He is One in His attributes, He is One in His actions, He is One in His orders, He is One in his justice for He is the Only source of the rewards for the good deeds and of retributions for the sins. He is the only One who has the fullest authority to declare what is lawful and what is not. He is the only One in all His beautiful names. He is, as the Qur'an reveals:

> *Say: He is Allah, the One and Only;*
> *Allah,the Eternal, the Absolute;*
> *He begets not, nor is He begotten;*
> *And there is none like unto Him.* (Qur'an, Ch. 112: 1-5).

67. *Al Ahadu*, The only One:

Allah is the unity in which all His attributes are united. He is the only Unique Being in whom His Oneness is not something that was created in time. His unity is truly devoid of having been created; and it is the highest form of expressing His essence. His unity can never be separated. He is the One to which another number cannot be given. This means that He is the only One to which numbers that follow the number one cannot be given. So, if I counted numbers after one, I would count the other number that follow one as two, three four, five etc., In Arabic I would say *waahid* (one), followed by *ithnayn* (two), followed by *thalaathah* (three), followed by *arba`a* (four), followed by *khamsah* (five) and so on. Not so, when I say *Ahad*. It also means "One" but the word *Ahad,* denoting "One", cannot be given any number to follow. There is no word for "two" after the word *Ahad.* The uniqueness of this number is that it cannot be separated, or broken apart, or multiplied. It means One and only One. That One is Allah. So, to show the uniqueness of this Attribute, we should again look at the following revelation:

Say: He is Allah, the One and Only;
Allah, the Eternal, Absolute;
He begets not, nor is He begotten;
And there is none like unto Him.

68. *As Samadu*, The Eternal:

Allah is the only one who is Eternal wand who is eternally besought in every need. To give an example of this Attribute of *Allah* let us say, that I feel ill, I will need to go to my doctor. If I need to learn something, I will need to refer to the books, to the teachers, to the colleges or universities. But in all these actions and other hundreds of actions that we do in our daily lives, I need to look separately for separate needs and separate requirements. Then again, there is no guarantee that the doctor will cure me. There is no guarantee that I will find what I am looking for in the libraries or colleges or universities. Not so with Allah. With Him, He is the one who I will seek for all my needs. He will cure me. The doctor may prescribe medication for me, but there is no guarantee that the medicine will cure me. My real recourse is only Allah. He is the only True support for me to rid myself of all the troubles and all the pains. It is through the attributes of Allah that we find His inexhaustible Treasures open and get distributed to all creatures. And so to explain completely this attribute of Allah together with the two attributes preceding this Attribute—*Al Waahidu, Al-Ahadu*—and this one, *As Samadu*, we should, one more time, refer to the following already quoted Chapter of Unity from the Qur'an:

Say: He is Allah, the One and Only;
Allah, the Eternal, Absolute;
He begets not, nor is He begotten;
And there is none like unto Him.

69. *Al Qaadiru*, The All-Powerful:

Allah is the Possessor of all the power. He is All-Powerful meaning He does what He wills, when He wills and what He wills. He needs no help and He creates *ex-nihillo*, from nothing. He is the Originator of all creation. *Al-Qadiru* is the One who does what He wills and if He wills, He does not do it. When He wills to do a thing, He says to it "Be" and it becomes. He does not need any tools, nor any model that He should follow. He created everything from nothingness and can return it to nothingness. It is all in His Hands and He has Power over everything. The universe is, as if a mirror of His Power exhibiting everywhere the total Power, the total Beauty, the total balance with which Allah. Allah has created everything,

only because He willed it. Also, it is not that once He has created, He
has no Power over it. He has fullest Power over it and can use what He
has created to establish the Sign of Him being *Al-Qadiru*. So, to give an
example, if He created the universe with all its physical properties and
laws, He can alter the physical laws any time if He wishes. If by physical
laws, water should hold the surface, He is Powerful to change this law as
He did by splitting open the sea so that Moses, could cross the sea with all
the children of Israel to safety. In the creation of a human being, Allah has
created him by breathing His Spirit in him. A human being also has power
over certain things, but his power is limited and is not absolute. Allah's
Power is infinite and is Absolute. He uses it if He wills it and if He does
not will it, He does not do it. In His wisdom, He may will it at a future date.
In His Hands is all good, and He is able to do everything.

70. *Al Muqtadiru*, The Bestower of all power:
Allah is the Bestower of all power. Without Him giving the power, nothing
can move. It is lifeless. Allah is the only source of all power. He creates,
and it is He who puts energy into it and gives it power. A man can think,
can move, can do things. This energy of thinking, moving about and doing
things from smallest to the biggest is only possible through the power
bestowed upon humankind by Allah. It is so with everything else. The
world moves, the planets, the cosmos in the heavens and all the movement
and all the growth and everything else exists and moves and grows only
because of the power bestowed upon them by Allah. So if we say sometimes
that humankind has been able to create and invent. Really speaking, too
a Muslim, this would be a false statement. The true statement to make
would be that through the power of thinking bestowed upon mankind by
Allah, mankind can think and invent a thing the raw material of which has
already been created and placed there for the benefit of humankind. All the
power comes only because Allah in His Attributes is *Al-Muqtadiru.*

71. *Al Muqaddimu*, The Expediter:
Allah in His Wisdom brings forward whomever He wills. Allah created
humankind and invited them to the Truth. Those who accept this Truth and
accept this blessed invitation to success, are led forward because Allah is
Al-Muqaddimu, the one who causes advancement. But there are others,
who, because Allah has bestowed humankind with the gift of free-will,
choose not to accept this Truth, in terms of faith, are left behind. Allah
also leads forward His servants whom He chooses to become the *Anbiya*
(prophets) and from the *Anbiya* some are advanced to become the *Rusul,*
(Messengers). The *Anbiya* and the *Rusul* help humankind to guide them

to the Truth. The advancement is in the Hands of Allah because He is *Al Muqaddimu.* He also advances love for someone in the hearts of others. And so, there are leaders among men who were advanced not only to lead others but also Allah advanced tremendous love for him in the hearts of others. In His Wisdom, Allah chooses and advances. As explained earlier, to a believer, In the hands of Allah is nothing but the good, and He has Power over everything.

72. *Al Muakkhiru,* The Delayer:

Allah in His Wisdom also retards one to progress, leaving one behind, delaying one's advancement. In this action, there is always a reason, leaving the slave to go through a test in this life. This test brings the slave close to Allah as what is required in this life is not only the *ibadah* but also the `ubudiyyah.* `Ibadah* means doing actions that are pleasing to Allah and `ubudiyyah* means to be pleased with what Allah wills. It is always important to know that we may be wishing for things to happen when we want them; but Allah knows when to fulfill our desires. A human being is weak and is hasty and is anxious for his desires to be fulfilled, but in Allah's plans, He knows exactly whether it is progression or regression if such desires were to be fulfilled at the time when the slave is asking for it. And so, if a believer is left behind in spite of his efforts, there may still be some good in it for him which he may not be realizing at the time. If he were to realize, he would understand that although he is behind the one who is ahead of him, there is someone who is behind him. In that sense, he is still ahead of someone. Allah knows in His Wisdom what is best for each of them.

73-74. *Al Awwalul Aakhiru,* The First, The Last:

Allah is The First. Now, when Muslims say Allah is The First, they mean that He is before the before. His being The First in no way relates to that which comes after Him. He is The First not in relation to something, which comes after Him. If we assumed that, it would mean that while He is The First, there is still second after Him. That is not the case at all. The fact is that He is uniquely One, as we saw in the Attribute of Him being *Al-Ahadu,* the One. He is *laysa kamithlihi Shay`un,* (there is nothing like Him) [81]. Here, in this Attribute it means that He is The First and there is nothing prior to Him. He is the Self-Existent. He exists by His own Essence. Everything else comes from Him and He is the only cause for everything else to become by His Decree of "Be!" and it becomes. Likewise, He is The Last. Everything else will perish and return to Allah. What will remain is Allah Himself. There is nothing after Him; neither is He after the after.

He is the Unique, He is the Eternal. His being the Ever-Living does not even mean that He has the Beginning, or that He was created or that He has the life-cycle of His own. His existence does not have two ends, the beginning and the ending. As we saw, He is before the before and He is The Last only in the sense that while everything else will have the end to its life-cycle and will return to Him. The only Being that will remain is Allah. He reveals:

> *All that is on earth will perish; but will abide (forever) the Face*
> *of Your Lord the Sustainer, Full of Majesty, Bounty and Honor.*
> (Qur`an, Ch. 55:26).

75. *Az Zaahiru*, The Manifest:

Allah is clearly manifest through our rational perceptions. He is also hidden (as we shall see in His next Attribute) who seek to see Him through their imaginations. Allah is also hidden in His endless, infinite Power and infinite Existence. Because He has no bounds, He cannot be imagined to have a shape or size and therefore He is invisible. He is hidden in His endlessness of being Omniscient, of His being Omnipotent, of His being Omnipresent, in His total infiniteness. He is, as the Qur'an reveals, the Light of the Heavens and the earth. Therefore, a bright light makes everything visible but in this enormous brightness becomes like a veil for anyone to else to see directly into the light. Instead, He is apparent in each and every thing that we see, we hear, we touch, we smell and taste. The attributes of God in the Monotheistic Faiths of Judeo-Christian and Islamic Traditions. Everything that we have, everything that we see or touch, is not Him but it is from Him. He is the One who has created and is therefore a proof of His existence and is dependent on Him for everything. So when you look at the piece of art, you will see the manifestation of an artist in that painting. It is as if the painting, if it were able to speak, will tell you that it is not me who is wonderful. I am just a mixture of colors that was lying in a tube or a container. It is the one who used me in this painting that is wonderful. I am just his manifestation. Allah is, therefore, manifest in everything that He has created. He manifests Himself in everything, the closest of which is an individual himself. As an individual yourself, you will see His Attributes. If one understands that, one appreciates the saying reported to be from the first Shi`a Imam `Ali: m*an `arafa nafsahu qad `arafa Rabbahu*, Whoever understood his own self has understood His Lord. Then look around you, and you will see the Signs of Allah everywhere. Now look up into the heavens and you will see His Signs, His manifestations, the complete cosmos, the manifestations of Allah every-where.

76. Al Baatinu, The Hidden:

Allah is, as we saw in His other attributes, the Manifest in His Signs within us and all around us, but His Essence is hidden from us. In the Signs within us and in the horizons, we know He is manifest, He is Present. He is hidden in His Essence but we know that we are the created ones; so there must be the Creator. So, my existence is the proof that He exists. He is, as we saw in the verse of the Throne that there is no god but He, the ever-living Allah and always with us wherever we may be. He, therefore exists. But we cannot fully comprehend simply because our minds are limited and can comprehend only in their limits and only within an area. We, with the finite capabilities can never understand the infinite. We are from Him but not Him. We know that Allah manifests Himself in all the Signs within us and around us but His Essence is hidden and we cannot fathom this because we are finite. A simple example of the reality of essence can be given by citing many examples in our everyday life. I heard a priest explain this phenomenon. Thus, he said, when you use your remote garage door opener, you press a button on your remote control and activate the motor mounted in the garage to open the garage door. Do you see the power that traveled from the remote control and entered through the closed garage door and activated the motor? Surely, you did not see anything travel from your remote control to the motor inside the closed garage door. But travel it did and activated the motor. You did not see it but it manifested itself by activating the machine so that you could open the garage door. Similar examples in our everyday life are the batteries, the television remote controllers etc., But perhaps the greatest example is our own self. The essence in our self is the life itself. We cannot see it but it is there. Its manifestation is the fact that you think, you move your limbs, and therefore you truly are. As a matter of fact, it is you essence. You cannot see it, but it manifests itself in yourself being alive and functioning. If this essence were to leave your body, you would no longer function. At that point, the life, the essence has departed and has left us nothing but a corpse.

A 10th. Century Muslim philosopher, Ibn Tufayl explained this in his book, *Hayy ibn Yaqzan,* in which he shows an abandoned boy in a remote island growing up amidst animals. Except for him, there are no other human beings on that island. The abandoned boy has been looked after by a deer and there is a motherly bonding between them. When the boy is in his teens, one day he finds his deer 'mother' is lifeless. The boy does not understand what has happened to her. There are no signs of any trauma on the body, no sign of any foul play by other animals. The boy, as he lovingly moves his hand over the dead body of this deer, feels the body feels soft below the diaphragm. Could it be something was in there that has escaped? He decides to cut open the body, finds a sharp stone and cuts open the body reaching the part that is hollow. He begins to think and concludes in his mind that the hollow part had something which has escaped. What was it? Now he thinks. In the evening, for the first time in his life, he looks up in the sky and begins to marvel at the moon and the stars. The beauty of the stars and the rising moon makes him think and conclude that there has to be some power that has created all this. The power that gives rise to the moon and the sun is the same power that took away his deer 'mother'. He concludes that power is Allah.

77. *Al Waali,* The Governor:
Allah is the One who manages the affairs of the whole universe, what is in them and what is between them. *Al-Waali* means the One who has charge over absolutely each and everything, in the whole universe. He is the Planner of things, He is the One who has Power over everything, He is the One who is the Activator of things. The governance of each and everything is in His control. For Him it is only to give an order "*koon,* Be!" and "*fa yakoon,* it becomes". But if this is how it begins and remains under the Governance of *Allah* its end is also in the hands of Allah. Its end is guaranteed and must come for everything has got a life-cycle of its own at the end of which it must return to Allah.

78. *Al Muta`ali,* The Most Exalted:
Allah is the Almighty, the Exalted one. This Attribute of Allah is the intensified form of *Al-`Aliyyu* and it means "The Most-Exalted One". Allah increases the provisions for His servants as their needs increase without decrease in anything with Allah. Whereas all His creation depreciates with time, because all creation have their own life-cycle at the end of which they die out, Allah Himself never decreases. On the contrary, in His attribute of being the Compassionate, the Merciful, He increases the provisions for His servants as He wishes. In our lives there are ups and downs, happiness and sadness, youthfulness and old age, health and sickness; nothing of any of these is for Allah. He is *Al-Muta`ali,* the Most-Exalted. At a society level, the societies have their own life-cycle and their own ups and downs. It is the same for dynasties and empires. They live through their life-cycle and then they decline and die out. What remains is just their history and some signs of the works they did and buildings they constructed which later lie in ruins. *Allah* in His Attributes has a record of deeds that individuals and societies and dynasties have done. It is this that really will matter in the

end. While we degenerate as our life-cycle depletes, Allah Himself is The Most Exalted, and is Ever-Living, the Eternal. In His Hands is the good, and He has the Power over everything in the Heavens and in the earth.

79. *Al Barru*, The Source of All-Goodness:

Allah is The Source of All-Goodness. He is The Beneficent, The Merciful. The Qur'an begins with this. We also know from the traditions of *Rasul-Allah (S)* (The Messenger) that Allah says His Mercy overtakes His Wrath. Allah does not create hardship for His servants. Humankind brings hardship upon themselves for their own selfish ends. Allah in His Mercy does not bring down punishment for the evil-doers at once. He gives them respite, time to realize and repent. If they repent and do good deeds, Allah blots out their sins. Not only does He blot out sins, for every good act, Allah reveals in the Qur'an, He multiplies the rewards ten times. In His Mercy towards His servants, if we do any wrong act, Allah does not multiply the punishment. A bad act is never punished for more than what it deserves, but the rewards for good act are multiplied ten-fold. A good act can be anything, even if it is just a smile to others. The doers of good bring themselves in the proximity of Allah. To achieve this status, one must show the faith in actions. Faith has to be accompanied by good actions. Allah is *Al-Barru*, the Perfect doer of all-good.

80. *At Tawwabu*, The Acceptor of Repentance:

Allah is *At-Tawwabu*, the One who constantly facilitates His servants to turn to Allah repenting. He does that by showing them some of His Signs, by awakening their hearts from the *ghaflat,* (heedlessness) into alertness as they see the manifestations of His existence around them. He promises them the Rewards for doing good; but also warning them of the dangers of the Retributions if they do not mend their ways. Thus, those hearts, which have understanding of this, turn to Allah repenting and seeking forgiveness. But there are those hearts that have turned to stone and no understanding can penetrate into them. For the believers, Allah in His compassion, reminds all His servants through the revelations. Theologians and scholars of Islam tell us that the hearts get awakened through the Qur'an. They say that one needs to understand the Qur'an to be truly guided from the state of sinfulness, where the conscious is not at rest, to the state of peace within one's own conscious where there is harmony with Allah's Will. In that situation, where one has truly repented to purify oneself, one is promised by Allah forgiveness. The Merciful Allah forgives, but the sin should be cleansed not only superficially but nipped from its bud. Allah loves forgiveness but Allah also wants to see the quality of forgiveness in His servants. Allah forgives and His Mercy is never doubted.

81. *Al Muntaqimu,* The Avenger:
Allah is of course the Forgiving and Merciful Nourisher, but if one persists in sinning and no warnings and no Signs from Allah changes one in one's arrogance, then Allah does eventually avenge such a person. This is the type of person who continued to revolt, oppressed others, was arrogant, faithless and ascribed partners to Allah. Nothing changed him to return to the path of good. This type of person finds himself smashed one day as he is thrown from the heights of his arrogance by the Divine Power of Allah brought down, totally smashed. In this, there are signs for others to save themselves.

82. *Al `Afuwwu,* The Total Forgiver, the Eraser of Sins:
Allah is The Eraser of sins. It is the intensive form and means to totally delete, or erase. In the previous attribute we saw that He is also The Avenger. This is absolutely necessary as a last resort. Allah's Mercy overtakes His Wrath and He continuously forgives. If one persists in one's sins and keeps on to one's arrogant ways and keeps oppressing and creating mischief on the earth, spilling blood and ruining lives of innocent people, it is only Just for Allah to avenge. He does this after having given time, respite for one to amend and reform. If one does reform and change ways to good, doing good deeds that are pleasing to *Allah* truly repenting for sins committed, Allah is not only *al-Ghafuru,* the Forgiver but also He is *Al-`Afuwwu,* The Eraser of sins. And His Bounties in the Hereafter cannot be compared to the bounties of this world, which are temporal and only a very small portion of the eternal and everlasting Bounties of Allah in the Paradise. A reformed life in Islam also requires the sinner to seek forgiveness from the people he caused hurt and injury. Only then can such a person expect to be forgiven. Muslim theologians explain this as a fundamental human right in Islam.

83. *Ar Raufu,* The Most Compassionate:
Allah is the most Compassionate. This attribute of Allah is the intense form of the one who takes pity on others. Allah is intensely Merciful and takes pity upon all His creatures; whether one is a Believer or not. Allah does not stop in His attribute of His Clemency, His Compassion. When we look at the creation of Allah we are filled with marvel at His creation, whether it is a monarch butterfly, who in spite of his flimsy wings can fly for thousands of miles, or a small silk-worm who produces silk, or a

honey-bee that produces honey in which there are benefits for humankind; one can never finish counting the clemency of Allah upon humankind. As explained before, Allah reveals:

> Say: *"If the ocean were ink (wherewith to count in writing) the words (bounties) of my Sustainer, sooner the ocean would be exhausted than would the words of my Sustainer, even if we added another ocean like it, for its aid.* (Qur'an, Ch. 18:109).

And again, in Chapter 31:27 we read:

> *And if all the trees on earth were pens and the ocean (were ink) with (other) seven oceans behind it to add to its (supply) yet would not the Words of Allah be exhausted (in the writing): for Allah is exalted in power, full of Wisdom.*

84. *Maaliku al-Mulku,* The Eternal Owner of Sovereignty:
Allah is the Eternal Owner of Sovereignty. His Sovereignty is Absolute and belongs only to Him. This is the fundamental Truth brought by all the prophets from Adam to *Rasul Allah* (The Messenger of Allah). Allah shares neither the Ownership nor the Power with any one. The guardianship of the universe belongs only to Allah.

> Say: *"Praise be to Allah who begets no son And has no partner in (His) Dominion Nor needs He any to protect Him from humiliation Yea, magnify Him for His greatness and glory* [82]

85. *Dhu al-Jalaali wa al-Ikraam,* The Lord of Majesty and Bounty:
Allah is the One to whom belongs all the Majesty and all the Bounty. There is no Majesty and there is no Honor that does not pertain to Allah. The Majesty is the Essence of Allah and The Honor. Everything emanates from Allah. Therefore, all honor that humankind has is bestowed upon humankind by Allah. Allah reveals:

> *And We have certainly honored the children of Adam; provided them with transport on land and sea, given them for sustenance things good and pure; And conferred on them special favors, above a great part of Our creation.* [83]

The truly Honorable one is only Allah. Through Him comes the honor. There is no creature that does not depend upon Him, The Lord of Majesty and Bounty.

86. *Al Muqsitu*, The Equitable:
Allah is the Up-holder of Equity. What it means is that Allah upholds fullest Justice for all (the oppressed and the oppressor) so that both are absolutely satisfied that the Justice has been done. Such equity is only possible with Allah. Nobody else can do that. The best example of this is in one of the *Ahadith* (traditions) where we are told that *Rasul Allah* (The Messenger of Allah) was thinking about something with a beautiful smile on his face. A companion asked him the reason for his smile and he replied by saying, "I see two men among my people who are in front of Allah, the Most High. One says, 'O Allah! Take from this man that which is rightfully mine'. Allah Most High tells the other man 'give your brother what rightfully belongs to him'. The usurper responds, "O Lord! I have no good deeds with which to repay this man'. Allah turns to the wronged one and says, "What should I do to your brother? He has nothing left to give you". The wronged man replies, "O Lord, let him take some of my sins." With tears in his eyes, Rasul Allah (S) said; "That is the Day of Last Judgment; that day is a day when each man will wish others to carry his sins." But he continued to relate and said: "After the wronged one has wished the usurper to take over some of his sins, Allah asks him to lift his head and look at the Paradise." The man looked up and said, "O Lord, I see cities of silver and palaces of gold bedecked with pearls. For which Prophet, which saint, which martyr are these palaces?" Allah Most High replied: "They are for those who can pay their price." The man who was wronged said, "Who can possibly pay their prices of these?" Allah replied, "Perhaps you could". The man asked, "How O Lord! I have nothing. What could I do to gain the price of the Paradise". Allah in His attribute of Al-Muqsitu replied, "By forgiving your brother, by giving up your claim in that which he took from you'. The wronged man said, "I forgive him, my Lord. I do not want my right". Allah in His immense Mercy said, "then hold the hand of your brother and enter my Paradise together".

Then Rasul Allah (S) said: "fear Allah and fear doing harm to each other and make peace among yourselves, for Allah Most High will make peace between the believers on the Day of Last Judgment".[84]

87. *Al Jaami`u*, The Gatherer: Allah is The Gatherer.
He gathers whatever He wishes, wherever He wishes. Allah brings together things that are similar, things that may not be similar, and things that are at variance with each other. Similarly, Allah will gather all humankind on the appointed Day, resurrecting them, although they may have become decomposed and dust in their graves or wherever they may be. If they were not buried but were cremated, Allah will bring them together from their ashes. He brings things together that we know of and things that we cannot even comprehend and cannot even know. It is He, the Exalted, who brought together the heavens and the earth, the stars and the planets, the earth and all that He created in it (the animals, the minerals, the vegetables) and gave them proportion and guidance. He is the one who brought our bones, nerves and brains and blood and millions of body cells together. It is He who brought together things that are opposites to each other. For example, heat and cold, fire and water, dryness and moisture. Likewise, He will bring us together on the Day of Resurrection to judge us. There is no doubt in it. Allah tells us in the Qur'an about those who are grounded in knowledge know this fact. He reminds us Himself and repeats in the Qur'an the beautiful supplication that those grounded in knowledge make to Allah:

> *Rabbana innaka Jaami`u Nnaasi li yawmin laa rayba fiihi*
> *Innallaaha laa yukhliful Mii`aad*

"Our Lord the Sustainer! You are He that will gather mankind together against a Date about which there is no doubt: for Allah never fails in His Promise".

88. *Al Ghaniyyu*, The Self-Sufficient:
Allah is the One who is the Richest. He is absolutely Self-Sufficient. The truest meaning of being absolutely self-sufficient, as in the case of Allah is that He is not dependent upon any one else for His being Self-Sufficient. In other words, He does not need to be enriched by someone or through his earnings to be rich. Allah the Exalted is above any connection with others. When someone needs to be enriched to become rich, he needs to earn that richness. Not so for Allah. His richness and His being Self-Sufficient is not dependent on any other source. He is the only One who is *Al-Ghaniyyu* because everything else is dependent upon Allah. No one can claim in this world for being rich by himself without being enriched by an action of his own work or earnings or by being bestowed of inheritance. That means

that had it not been for that means, he could not be rich. Allah does not need any means. He is the One who is self-sufficient in the truest sense of the word. Allah is independent in His riches; but everybody else depends on Him.

89.   *Al Mughniyyu*, The Enricher:
Allah is The Enricher. He is the One who satisfies the needs of others, as all are totally dependent of Him. He is The Provider, He is The Maintainer, He is The Nourisher, He is The Sustainer of the Universe. He may grant abundant riches to any one and some are rendered poor. It is all in the Hands of Allah. But each one has a purpose. In each state, there is a test. The rich has a duty to help those who are less fortunate in the society. The rich has to know that what he has been bestowed with is pure blessings form Allah. In what he has been bestowed with, there is a clear share of those who are less fortunate. The poor need not remain in the state of poverty. Allah has put a test on such a person of not only to be patient but to continuously endeavor to change his condition from being poor to being self-sufficient; but at the same time, both the rich and the poor have to know that the true Self-Sufficient is only Allah because He is independent of others whereas everybody else depends on Him. Material riches are a blessing from Allah. One does the *shukr* (gives thanks) to Allah for this favor by fulfilling the duty towards those who are less fortunate than one is. But the greatest gift from Allah is the gift of wisdom. A wise man is the one who has the fear of Allah in him all the time. A wise man is pious and does nothing to displease Allah. A wise man may be materially rich or he may be materially poor; but although materially poor, he would still be the richest if he is blessed with wisdom. To such a person, not being materially wealthy will not grieve him and he will continue with his pursuits and Allah may change his condition because Allah is *Al-Mughniyyu*, The Enricher. The other gift from Allah is the gift of `*ilm* (knowledge, or learning). A learned person knows all that is stated in the above paragraph. But he also knows that while material wealth depreciates with spending, the knowledge increases as it is spent more and more. In any state, though, a believer will always be conscious that whatever he has, is from Allah and whatever he does with his life, he is accountable for it on the Day of Resurrection for the Judgment against him or in favor of him.

90.   *Al Maani`u*, The Preventer:
Allah is The Preventer. He prevents us from the sufferings and pains that would come to us had He not prevented the causes of pains and sufferings in the first place. As human beings we wish for endless things. In the

fulfillment of some of those wishes there may be harm to us. We would not know about the harm until the actual wish is fulfilled. Allah is the only One who knows and in His love And in His Mercy He prevents a thing happening. Allah reveals:

> "... it is possible that you dislike a thing which is good for you and that you love a thing which is bad for you. But Allah knows and you do not know" (Qur'an, Ch. 2:216).

Scholars in Islam, explaining this, tell usthat if we do not get what we wish, it is not because Allah has not heard our prayers to Him, or that He does not know what we wish. He knows even the lurking thoughts of our minds and He is *Al-Ghaniyyu* The Rich, and He is *Al-Khabiru* The Knower of everything. In His attributes He knows the future results of everything. If in granting our wishes, there is harm for us, Allah is the One who prevents from fulfilling that wish. Many time, we do realize that had our wish been realized and fulfilled, it would have brought for us bad results and we thank Allah from having prevented our wish from happening at the time.

91. *Ad Dhaarru*, The Distresser:
Allah has given mankind a free will and has shown mankind clear criterion between right and wrong, between good and bad. He did that because He has not forsaken mankind. Allah sent continuous prophets and messengers and gave them scriptures and clear criterion between right and wrong. Allah has put the capacity in humankind so that one knows when one is committing an ugly act or is sinning, something within oneself, referred to as the *Nafsu lawwamah* (the haunting conscious) tells one that this is a wrong act. If one still persists in doing this, Allah will let one because Allah has already ordained free will upon humankind. Allah has willed upon human beings the free will as a test for mankind and Allah watches whether they obey the commands of Allah and refrain from ugly acts. If the one chooses to continue living the life full of sin and immorality, one will bring upon the distress upon oneself. Allah has created human beings so that they should be progressive, and good, and should know Allah, and worship Him. If any still chooses evil, there are safety valves built within him that will tell him through that inner voice each and every one of us carries, that the act is wrong. If one persists, that is the distress one has invited upon oneself, not from Allah. It was one's choice. If one chooses distress, Allah will grant it. If he turns repentant, Allah in His Mercy, forgives sins if the repentance is sincere.

92. *An Naafi`u,* The Creator of Good:

Allah is the creator of good and pure. Mankind is His best creation and Has been is appointed as His Vicegerent on the earth. Allah the Exalted, then gave him intellect. He gave him conscious and the ability to decipher between good and bad, between justice and injustice. This in order so that humankind should understand and be thankful to Allah. Humankind should endeavor in this life to be compassionate and kind in the Kingdom of Allah and act as His vicegerent. This he can do by establishing, first in his life, the rule of Allah. He should be kind, compassionate, benevolent towards others, but also very careful he does not overstep his authority in this world. Allah reveals:

> *"And We have certainly honored the children of Adam; provided them with Transport on land and sea, given them for sustenance things good and pure; And conferred on them special favors, above a great part of Our creation"*

93. *An Nuru,* The Light:
In the Qur'an, Allah also describes Himself as the Light of the heavens and the earth:

> *"Allah is the Light of the heavens and the earth . . ."* [85]

Everything that exists in the heavens and the earth points to its Creator, Allah. The light can be called to be worthy of light only when it brings out things that are nonexistent because they are into dark, into existence by the light. Allah's Light shines upon all His creation making it visible. Allah is free from the darkness of non-existence. He is the Light. His Light is the Light of His Essence. Since there cannot be anything when the light shines upon it; and the source that brought it out is the light that shone on it, so also there is nothing in the heavens or the earth, what is in them and what is between them that does not point to its Creator as the source who created it, proportioned it, guided it and nourished it; and above all, gave it a life-cycle of its own. Human beings have been given intelligence to ponder over the Signs of Allah within them and in the universe through the light of faith. Through this light the good becomes visible from evil and right from wrong. Those who have this faith feel clearly in their life that Allah becomes their *wali* (friend) and removes them from the darkness into the light. This light shows them the straight path in which there is a guaranteed salvation. It eliminates the darkness of ungratefulness and sins rendering and promoting the life of goodness and purity into the salvation.

94. *Al Haadi,* The Guide:

Allah is the Guide. He promised guidance to mankind when Nabi Adam and Bi*bi Hawwa* (Adam and Eve) were asked to go down on to the earth after they ate from the forbidden tree. Allah promised, in His attribute as the Guide that He will not forsake mankind. He sent continuous guidance to humankind in the form of the Prophets He chose to guide humankind. His Promise is amply fulfilled. Allah sent guidance. Prophets, Messengers, Messengers of the Resolve, right down to the final Prophet, the Messenger of Allah and the Seal of the Prophets were raised by Allah to guide the humankind. Further, it is Allah who guides whomever He wishes to the Knowledge of His Essence. This is known as the *Ma'arifah* (Gnosis). Allah does not create anything without purpose and without guiding so that the created uses that guidance in order to understand His Essence. He creates, proportions and guides. This is for all creatures. For a human being, Allah has also made available to him the free-will. Through the free-will, man can choose freely whether to be guided or misguided. Man has at his disposal all the fundamental guidance through all the prophets that Allah sent; but also a human being carries within himself a special *fitrah,* which points him towards his Creator. But should he choose to be misguided and accepts misguidance, Allah will let him be misguided. Allah does not wish evil. He created man in the best mould; but the free will in man lets him choose evil and thus become of the misguided one. In His attribute as the Guide, Allah has guided all his creatures to acquire means for their existence through this life and has created for each thing a life-cycle of its own. Exalted is *Allah* the Compassionate, the Merciful.

95. *Al Badi'u,* The Originator:

Allah is The Originator par Excellence. He is the cause of all creation. He creates *ex Nihillo*. It means that He creates from nothing. He does not need any planning, any tools, any plan, any guide. He creates by Himself. He is the one who is *al badi'u ssamaawaati wa al ardhi,* the Originator *ex Nihillo* of the heavens and the earth. *He is laysa ka mithlihi shayun*. That is to say, there is nothing like Him. There was nothing before Him, so there is nothing like Him. He is the only One, the Unique. His creation is also unique for there is wonder and marvel in everything that He creates and no two things that He creates are equal. Each one carries its own signature, its own stamp. No two finger prints are alike. People may resemble each other but they are different from each other. Allah creates, proportions, guides and gives it a life-cycle of its own, as already explained. His uniqueness was expressed by the early caliphate in the history of Islam. Someone showed the chessboard to the early Caliph marveling at a small, square board, yet men can play thousands of games on it. The early Caliph asked him to look at the face of a man. Although smaller than a chess board the marvel is that no two faces are alike although all faces have two eyes, a nose, mouth, ears etc., in the same place, they are never alike. Each has its own expression. It is like a never ending kaleidoscope of expressions, that goes on forever. Everything that human beings have been able to discover and create is never original. It is only discovered. So, in the history of humankind if man was first the food gatherer, not a producer of food, there was someone who had already put food for him. Likewise, when mankind later become food producers, there was someone who had already put seeds there for them to sow and grow. The growth itself is not possible if Allah had not created the Sun and the Moon and had not sent rains from the skies. Glory belongs only to Allah.

96. *Al Baaqi,* The Everlasting:
Allah is the Only One who is everlasting. Everything else is limited by time and has a life-cycle of its own. In the end, it must perish. Allah is Ever-living. Death does not overtake him. Neither is He subject to time. Time itself is created by Allah and it is moving fast toward the Day of Judgment. Allah is before the before and He is Eternal. This means that He will be after the after. Allah is the only Sovereign who is not affected by time and this will become as clear as the daylight on the Day of Accounting when all mankind will be raised for accounting of their deeds on the earth during their lifetime. Allah is, was, and will always remain the only Everlasting Lord and the only Sovereign. Allah reveals:

> *All that is on earth will perish; But will abide (forever) The Face of your Lord,—Full of Majesty, Bounty and Honor.*[86]

97. *Al Waarithu,* The Supreme Inheritor:
Allah is the supreme Inheritor. We have seen in the attributes of Allah already described that everything belongs to Him. Everything that we have has come to us because of Him. But in the truest sense, we do not own anything. Humankind is the steward of Allah on the earth. If Allah gives him more, it does not become his. It is only Allah's favors upon the man that he has been given more. So what is expected of him is to thank and be grateful to Allah for having granted him with more and to understand that there is a test for him in what he has been given. The test is to give

from what he has been given by Allah to others who have less than he has. In other words, almsgiving, the *zakat* (annual required almsgiving from savings) and the *Sadaqaat* (extra charity). In the end, whatever he has, has to go back to the original giver, the true Inheritor. One may be very rich on this earth and may have been granted all kinds of wealth and in enormous quantity; and he may then preserve it and transfer it to his children upon death. This may go on for generation, a Grace from Allah and also a test as to how the wealth was used, but in the end, everything will return to Allah and He alone will be the Supreme Inheritor of everything. Allah reveals:

> It is We who will inherit the earth
> And all beings thereon: to us they
> Will all be returned.[87]

It was His in the first place. One may be the "King" on this earth, but it is only temporary because when he dies, he is in level with everyone else because death is the leveler. The true Kingdom belongs only to Allah. Allah reveals a scenario in the Qur'an in regards to this. On the Day of Accounting when all will be raised and face the Day of Accounting, Allah will ask:

> To whom belongs the Kingdom this Day?
> To Allah the One, the Dominating One

In the opening chapter of the Qur'an, Muslims read as part of their Five daily prayers, these words:

> I begin in the name of Allah The All-Merciful, The Compassionate
>   (All the) Praise(and Glory) belongs to the
>   Sustainer of the Universe
>   Most Gracious Most Merciful
>   King of the Day of Judgment
>   You alone do we worship
>   And Your Help do we seek
>   Guide us to the Straight Path
>   The path of those upon whom You have bestowed Your Grace
>   Not those whose portion is Wrath
>   And not those who have gone astray.

98. *Ar Rashidu*, The Guide to the Right Path:

Allah is All-Merciful, the Compassionate, the Nourisher. In His Mercy, Allah is the Guide to the Right Path, the Path that leads to a guaranteed salvation. He leads perfectly. There is no fault in His leading and completing of all affairs. He is the Guide who does not need anybody to guide Him or any counselor to counsel Him. He is Allah, the Exalted, the Most High. Everything that Allah has created is guided by Him. In the case of humankind, Allah has bestowed him with the freewill. Man uses this freewill to become a guide but this is dependent entirely and only to the extent that he is guided. Allah does not enforce upon humankind His teachings He sent through His chosen prophets in the history of humankind. Allah guided mankind to the Right Path by sending Prophets to all nations in their own languages. The prophets taught what was revealed to them but were asked not to enforce the teachings. Allah, instead of enforcing His Laws upon humankind, left humankind free to choose for themselves the right from the wrong and gain immense rewards from Allah by choosing the right path. The finality of this path for mankind is the Qur'an in which there is the guidance for the humankind and clear criterion between the right and the wrong.

99. *As Saburu*, The Patient:

Allah is the Patient One. He times all things perfectly. The Patient is one whom haste cannot rush to do things prematurely. Allah's plans are not delayed beyond their appointed time and they are not hastened. Allah brings about things in their appropriate time. Here again Allah's Mercy overtakes His Wrath. Allah could bring about the punishment upon the sinners as soon as the sin is committed, but Allah is Patient. He gives respite for us to repent and turn to Him. If we do, He is Forgiving, the Merciful and forgives in His Mercy. Likewise, He does not delay anything beyond the appointed time.

CHAPTER FOUR:
THE STATUS OF JESUS IN THE JEWISH TRADITION.

In the Jewish tradition, Jesus is neither the son of God, nor God himself. Jesus is also neither the Messiah[88] nor the divinely inspired prophet.

God in the Jewish tradition is only One. The scriptures clearly specify this. For example, Deuteronomy 6:4-5 reads,

> "Hear O Israel: The Lord our God is one Lord; and you shall love the Lord your God with all your heart, and all your soul and all your might".

Loving the Lord with all "heart and soul and might" means adhering to this tenet fully and not accepting any notion that the Lord God can be divisible; or any notion that the Lord God has any associates or partners. The sacredness of this fundamental law is seen also in the other Jewish scripture, the Talmud. The Talmud specifies that any man who claims to be the God is a liar. This sacredness, which also shared by Islam, is because associating God with anybody else would tantamount to idolatry; and idolatry is a major Sin.

The Jewish tradition does not accept Jesus even as the Messiah because Jews do not believe Jesus fulfilled the Messianic prophecies revealed in the Hebrew Bible. The Jewish Messiah is the one who will arise to bring about the messianic age. According to the Jewish scriptures, the true Messiah will be the redeemer of Jews,[89] he will fight holy wars for God so that there will be an era of peace on the earth.[90] The other stumbling block in considering Jesus the Messiah is that a Jewish Messiah has to be born of human parents and must be from the descendant of David, and must not possess supernatural qualities of Jesus.[91]

In the Rabbinic tradition of the Talmudic times, Jesus is not even considered to be the "divinely appointed" prophet. A true prophet in the Jewish tradition must not speak only about the God of Israel as the true

God, but must also not diverge from anything that is already revealed by the God of Israel. Even if such a person performed super natural miracles, he still cannot be considered divinely inspired because it would not make sense to perform super natural miracles while denying what the God of Israel has already revealed. Sources tell us that for

> ". . . two thousand years, Jews rejected the claim that Jesus fulfilled the messianic prophecies of the Hebrew Bible, as well as the dogmatic claims about him made by the church fathers—that he was born of a virgin, was the son of God, was part of a divine Trinity, and was resurrected after his death. Thus, any divergence from the tenets of Biblical Judaism espoused by Jesus would disqualify him from being considered a prophet in Judaism. This was the view adopted by Jesus' contemporaries, as according to rabbinical tradition". This tradition is stated also in the Jewish Talmud. In the Jewish faith, the prophecy ended when Malachi died. As Malachi lived centuries before Jesus it is clear that the rabbis of Talmudic times did not view Jesus as a divinely inspired prophet"(see "Judaism's View of Jesus" in Wikipedia, The Free Encyclopedia).

It is interesting to note, however, that because of these reasons, not only Jesus but also others who also claimed to be the Messiah, men like Shabbatai Tezvi, and Bar Cochba are also rejected in their claims of Messiah.

For the Jewish Tradition, the Biblical prophecies must come to pass exactly as revealed. The Messiah must usher an age that will bring about recognition of God and an Age of Perfection which will clearly demonstrate the universal peace.[92]

Also, a Jewish Messiah will not be born of a virgin birth. According to the Jewish Tradition "the Christian idea of a virgin birth is derived from the verse in Isaiah 7:14 describing an 'alma' as giving virgin birth. The world 'alma' has always meant a young woman, but Christian theologians came centuries later and translated it into 'virgin'. This accords Jesus birth with a first century pagan idea of mortals being impregnated by gods".[93]

The Jewish Tradition also does not accept Isaiah chapter 53 referring to Jesus as the "suffering servant". The Jewish Tradition (and the Islamic Tradition shown in the following chapter) strongly believe in the only God who is incorporeal. That is to say, the God without any physical features.

CHAPTER FIVE:
THE STATUS OF JESUS (`ISA IBN MARYAM—JESUS, SON OF MARY) IN THE ISLAMIC TRADITION.[94]

The status of Jesus in Islam is a fascinating account. Jesus is considered in Islam to be the Messiah. He is the Rasul,(the Messenger) of God who brought clear guidance for the Children of Israel showing them clear distinction between right and wrong.

Jesus is mentioned twenty-five times in the Qur'an and is shown as a very special prophet born of a virgin mother, Maryam (Mary). A complete chapter 19 of the Qur'an is revealed in her name. The chapter reveals the account of how Mary was approached by the angel Gabriel giving her news of the birth of Jesus and how God has raised the status of Jesus from the time of his birth. The Qur'an shows Jesus revealed God's word even from the cradle proclaiming these words, as revealed in the Qur'an:

> "He (Jesus) said (from the cradle): 'I am indeed a servant of Allah: He has given me revelation and made me a Prophet. And He has made me blessed wheresoever I be, and has enjoined on me Prayer and Charity as long as I live. (He) has made me kind to my mother, and not overbearing or miserable. So peace is on me the day I was born, the day that I die, and the day that I shall be raised up to life (again)" [95]

The chapter goes on to declare that this statement is the statement of truth

> "about which they dispute. It is not befitting to (the majesty of) God that He should beget a son. Glory be to Him! When He determines a matter, He only says to it "Be" and it is. Verily Allah is my Lord and your Lord: therefore worship ye only Him: this is (the only) way that is Straight". [96]

The concept of prophet hood demands from Muslims to believe in all the biblical prophets and to believe in all the previous revelations.[97] Muslims make no difference amongst prophets of the past, albeit with the belief that each prophet came with a particular status accorded to him and was given clear Signs from God. Not all prophets came with the same status as that of Jesus and Jesus is the only one shown in the Qur'an born of a virgin mother. Further, Jesus is the only one shown in the Qur'an who will return in the last days to establish the Kingdom of God on the earth:

> *"And (Jesus) shall be the Sign (of the coming of) the Hour (of Judgment); therefore have no doubt about the (Hour), but ye follow Me; this is a Straight Way".[98]*

Belief in all the prophets is a fundamental requirement in Islam. The Qur'an declares:

> *"Say ye: We believe in God and the revelation given to us and to Abraham, Ismail, Issac, Jacob and the Tribes, and that given to Moses and Jesus, and that given to (all) prophets from their Lord: we make no difference between one and another of them: and we bow to God (in Islam).[99]*

The Prophet is reported to have been asked once by a Christian group from a nearby city of Najran in Saudi Arabia. The Christian delegate had come to learn the exact state of Jesus in Islam. They argued how can Jesus be only the Prophet of God (and not the Son) when his was a miraculous birth of a virgin mother. The Qur'an shows God revealed a reply this question immediately:

> *"The similitude of Jesus before God is that of Adam: He created him from dust, then said to him "Be": and he was. The Truth (comes) from God alone; so be not of those who doubt".[100]*

That is to say that if God can create Adam without the father or the mother, merely from the dust, why should it be difficult to believe that God can create only from the mother.

The story of Jesus and Mary is revealed in the Qur'an in various chapters. Each time Jesus is shown the Prophet who came with special powers to heal the sick, to give life to the dead and to tell what people were hoarding in their homes. But each of these miracles has a proviso bi idhnillahi, ('only' with the permission of Allah). Jesus's message in more than one place in the Qur'an is shown as one fundamental teaching:

> *"verily, God is my Lord and your Lord. Therefore worship Only Him. That is the (only) Straight Path".*[101]

During his earthly mission, Jesus is also shown as prophesying the advent of the Prophet Muhammad. In the Qur'an we read:

> *"And remember, Jesus, the son of Mary, said: "O Children of Israel! I am the Messenger of God (sent) to you, confirming the Law (which came) before me, and giving glad Tidings of a Messenger to come after me, whose name shall be Ahmad . . . "*[102]

Islam does not believe Jesus was crucified. They believe Jesus was raised alive, is alive in the heavens and as already indicated above, Islam believes Jesus will return in the Last Days and will establish Kingdom of God. Jesus will fight the Dajjal (Antichrist) and will defeat him ushering into the era of Peace on the earth and worship of only Allah.[103]

In one passage the Qur'an shows Jesus with his disciples in the Last Supper followed by a passage in which Jesus will be asked on the Day of Judgment this:

> *And behold! God will say: "Oh Jesus the son of Mary! Did you say to men, 'worship me and my mother as gods in derogation of God'?" He will say: "Glory to you! Never could I say what I had no right (to say). Had I said such a thing, you would indeed have known it. You know what is in my heart, though I do not know what is in yours. For You know in full all that is hidden. Never said I to them anything except what You commanded me to say; for example: 'worship God, my Lord and your Lord'; And I was a witness over them whilst I dwelt amongst them; when You took me up, You were the Watcher over them, and You are a Witness to all things".*[104]

CONCLUSION

One of the most important things argued in this book is the existence of God and the relationship we as human beings have with God. The relationship we as human beings have with God is the relationship of love. I have argued, that in proving the existence of God, it is a false notion to think that we can arrive to correct conclusions only if we can verify with our empirical experiences; or if we can verify with our sensual perceptions of seeing, tasting, smelling, hearing or touching. To arrive at the conclusion with utmost certainty is to use all of the above sensual perceptions accompanied by rational perceptions; because it has been proven many times that a thing unseen does not mean it does not exist. Philosophers and thinkers in the past have thought very deeply about this and have arrived at proper conclusion that sensual perceptions must be accompanied by rational perceptions to arrive at the most certain correct conclusion. In the time of Plato, he explained this phenomenon through the 'allegory of a cave' discussed in this book. Other thinkers in different cultures used their own methods to explain clearly and succinctly the fact of relationship between sensual and rational perceptions to arrive at the truth. In the modernity we live in, this is not difficult to understand. We use all kinds of remote gadgets that are totally wireless and they make our world run.

The attributes of God discussed in this book, and believed by all the three monotheistic faiths of Judaism, Christianity and Islam, show God as the existing God and is absolutely Compassionate and loving God. The attributes of God reveal that God loves us more than a mother loves her child. In this relationship, God is not only the loving, giving, forgiving God; He is also the Sovereign Lord. His uniqueness is also that He, although the Sovereign and the Sustainer of the universe, He in His Lordship is neither a tyrant nor a corrupt God.

Since all this has already been stated, all I need to do now is to briefly restate that we, as human beings, need to nurture this relationship by reciprocrating this compassion and love God has for us. One of the greatest ways to reciprocate this love is by being compassionate and loving to all our fellow human beings.

God, as we have seen in His attributes, does not restrict His love only for the Muslims, Jews or Christians alone. The 'holier than thou' attitude is not an attribute of compassion and love. The 'holier than thou' attitude is not an attribute reflecting the image of God in which we as human beings have been created. I think the monotheistic faiths, since collectively they represent the majority of human population have a duty to reject any notion promoted by the Twenty-first century prophets of doom and gloom for this world. If we were to reciprocate the attributes of love planted in our hearts by truly nurturing it and manifesting it in our daily lives, we would reject any notion of the clash of civilizations. Equally and emphatically, we would also reject any ideology that nurtures and promotes hatred towards others. What we need to do is to bring about a special kind of revolution in our life. I call it an 'intellectual revolution'. This revolution demands rejection of extremism, whether fuelled by the ideas of the far-right, or the ideas of religious fanaticism, in any way, shape and form. Any ideology of violence really belongs to the dustbin of history. No ideology of violence in the history has ever succeeded and no religion in its truest sense teaches violence.

God is known by several names. Whether one calls Him Allah or YHVH, or Adonai, or Elohim or any of the several names, God is One and is the same God with all His attributes, as loving as ever, discussed in this book.

(Endnotes)

1 See http://dictionary.reference.com/browse/God.

2 At-Tabatabai, al-Allamah as-Sayyid Muhammad Husayn, Al-Mizan: An Exegesis of the Qur'an, (Wofis Publishers, Iran, 1983), p.25.

3 Qur'an, 112:1-5. See also Ayoub, Muhammad, Islam: Faith and History, (Oxford Publications, England, 2004), p.46.

4 Ibid., pp.46-7.

5 Maimonides was one of the most famous 12th. century Jewish philosophers who found refuge in the court of Muslim ruler Salah Din (known in the West as Saladin) from where he wrote important treatises.

6 Tozer, A. W., Knowledge of the Holy, (Harper Collins, New York, 1961), p.1-3.

7 In Ch. 61:6 of the Qur'an, Jesus is recorded to have prophesied of the coming of the Prophet of Islam, Muhammad. The words are: And remember, Jesus, the son of Mary, said: "O Children of Israel! I am the Messenger of God (sent) to you, confirming the Law (which came) before me, and giving glad Tidings of a Messenger to come after me, whose name shall be Ahmad." See The Qur'an, Tr. by Abdullah Yusuf Ali.

8 Qur'an referring to the return of Jesus. This will be the Sign of last days. See Qur'an. 43:61.

9 See Genesis. Muslims are from the progeny of Ishmael, Abraham's first born. Scholars put all these three traditions as the Western traditions in their textbooks. See Oxtoby, Willard G., World Religions: Western Traditions. See also Lings Martin, Muhammad: His Life Based on Earliest Sources. Interesting biography post 9/11 is also written by Armstrong Karen, Muhammad: A Biography of The Prophet. See also article on "Islam" by Esposito, John L.; Fasching, Darrel J. and Lewis Todd, in World Religions Today.

10 For example, see Qur'an, 56:1-6.

11 Laysa ka mithlihi shay'un.(There is nothing whatever like unto Him. Qur'an, 42:11).

12 Tozer, p.28.

13 Qur'an, Ch. 6:76-79.

14 Qur'an, Ch. 88:17-20.

[15] See Confucius: The Analects. A collection of the sayings of Confucius who was a great teacher in the ancient Far East.

[16] See Chandogya Upanishad, 6:2. Section 13.

[17] Muzaffar, M. Rida, The faith of Shi`a Islam, (The Muhammadi Trust, London, 1982), p.1

[18] Robert Diffinbaugh, Let Me See Thy Glory: A Study of the Attributes of God,(Biblical Studies Press, Texas, 1997), p.8. (See also bible.org /series/ let-me-see-thy-glory-study-attributes-god).

[19] Qur'an: Ch. 7:143.

[20] Tozer, p.11.

[21] Ibid., p.11.

[22] Ibid., p.14.

[23] See http://dictionary.reference.com/browse/Tetragrammaton, "The Hebrew word for god, consisting of the four letters yod, he, vav, and he, transliterated consonantally usually as YHVH, now pronounced as Adonai or Elohim in substitution for the original pronunciation forbidden since the 2nd or 3rd century b.c.".

[24] 'Elohim' is a standard Hebrew term for God with the letter 'G' spelt in upper-case. See also Isaiah, 45:22.

[25] 'Immanuel' appears 2 times in the Hebrew Bible (see Isaiah, 7:141 and Isaiah, 8:8) and one time in the New Testament in Matthew,1:23. For Christians, this is the fulfillment of the prophecy in the advent of Jesus.

[26] Some scholars believe the name 'Jehovah' is a hybrid combining Latin letters JHVH with the vowels of 'Adonai'. See 'Jehovah' in Wikipedia.

[27] See for example, www.allaboutgod.com.

[28] See http://dictionary.reference.com/browse/Tetragrammaton, "The Hebrew word for god, consisting of the four letters yod, he, vav, and he, transliterated consonantally usually as YHVH, now pronounced as Adonai or Elohim in substitution for the original pronunciation forbidden since the 2nd or 3rd century B.C.".

[29] Tozer, pp.2-3.

[30] Allah is simply an Arabic word translates into English as God. The name Allah has been in use since pre-Islamic times in the ancient Near East (now the Middle East). The grammatical uniqueness of this word is that in its etymological meaning, it means only one thing, "to worship".

[31] This is the first line of the two-line Islamic Creed. The uniqueness of the Islamic Creed is that it begins with the negation "There is no God except Allah". This negates any possibility to ascribe any partners to God. He is the only One to be worshipped. The second line in the Creed is "Muhammad is the Messenger of Allah".

[32] Qur'an, Ch. 2:255. This is the 'Throne Verse' in the Qur'an. Muslims often mention "High and Exalted is He" when they mention the name Allah.

[33] Qur'an, Ch. 57:1. There is absolutely nothing that is hidden from God. He has knowledge of the minutest thing in the universe. In the Islamic belief human beings are totally transparent and can hide nothing from God.

[34] Chapter 112 in the Qur'an sums up the essence of God in Islam. He is the unique One. No other number can come after the word Ahad in Arabic.

[35] See Shomali, Mohammad Ali (ed). God: Existence and Attributes (Institute of Islamic Studies, London, 2008),pp.12-13.

[36] Qur'an, Ch.19:65. is explicit in the declaration of God that His Mercy overtakes His Wrath. Qur'an also reveals that God rewards ten times for any good act. Bad acts are punishable to the extent of the bad act.

[37] See Sheikh Tosun B. al-Halveti, The Most Beautiful Names, (Threshold Books, Vermont, U.S.A., 1985),pp.5-6.Hadith al-Qudsi refers to those prophetic traditions that were divinely revealed to the Prophet.

[38] Qur'an, Ch.7:180.This is the first verse of the Qur'an confirming Allah's attributes, the all-Merciful, the all-Compassionate. All the chapters (except Chapter 9) begin with this verse.

[39] Qur'an, Ch:7:156. In the attribute of Ar-Rahman Allah is seen as all-Merciful to all His creatures, whether they are believers or not.

[40] Traditions that came directly from Allah to Prophet Muhammad. These traditions may not necessarily be part of the verses in the Qur'an but if the Prophet began with the words "Allah says or Allah said", anything the Prophet said following these words is considered the tradition of the highest excellence.

[41] The Qur'an has a total of 114 chapters. All except one (Ch. 9) begin with this invocation. This verse at the beginning of chapters has the Name Allah and two of His attributes. While the attribute of Ar Rahman guarantees Allah's mercies to all, believers and non-believers in their earthly life, the attribute of Allah's all-Compassion will apply only to those who will be rewarded with the paradise.

[42] The uniqueness of this attribute shows God's Mercy encompasses both believers as well as non-believers in their earthly lives.

[43] This attribute shows Mercy of Allah in its highest form in the Hereafter reserved for those who led the righteous lives in their earthly life. The fundamental condition of righteousness are actions of kindness and mercy to all. Allah (God) loves acts of charity.

[44] Righteousness in Islam is not through Faith alone. Faith must be accompanied with good deeds. The fundamental requirement for good deeds is compassion and charity towards others. There are many verses

in the Qur'an explaining this. Muslim exegetes show among many verses, verse 177 in Chapter 2 of the Qur'an.

[45] Qur'an, Ch.3:26.

[46] Allah's power is clearly manifest in our lives. Our life-cycle is fully in the hands of God. In spite of all the progress humankind has made, we have not been able to solve the mystery or the cure of ageing, or the death that must come. God has the power to bring low those who are arrogant tyrants, or raise the status of those who are weak. For Muslims everything in the heavens and earth glorifies Allah. Allah is Total perfection, there is nothing negative in Him. The modern totally unjustified extremism is not because Muslims think they are greater than God; but the extremism itself shows their motivations are political oriented and results in total disregard for the laws of Allah. In that sense, Muslims are guilty of blasphemy because nowhere in the Islamic theology violence perpetrated by Muslim extremists is ever. justified. See Qur'an, 5:32.

[47] Qur'an, Ch.59:23.

[48] Qur'an, Ch.36:58.

[49] Allah is the Guardian of faith. Believers find comfort knowing as they go through their earthly life that Allah watches over them and guards them.

[50] Qur'an, Ch.59:23.

[51] Qur'an, Ch.2:129.

[52] The early Caliph of Muslims, Ali b. Abu Talib, is also the first Imam of Shi`a Muslims. He was the first intellectual thinker of Islam. See a Sunni Scholar's research work on him in his book, Imam Ali Ibn Abi Talib: The First Intellectual Muslim Thinker. By Dr. Muhammad Abdu Rauf.

[53] The verb SH-T-N in Islamic mean to have gone astray, far from the truth. Shaytan (one who is far away from the truth) is a noun, conjugated form of this verb. It is interesting to note that Seeking protection from the evil forces is a fundamental requirement in Islam. The Qur'an asks believers to seek refuge in Allah from the cursed shaytan or Satan (who is declared in the Qur'an as the open enemy of mankind). Allah's gift to mankind is the protection from all kinds of Satanic and other destructive forces in the earthly life of mankind. Allah provides this security because, as we see in His attributes He is al-Mu'minu, The Guardian of Faith; al-Muhayminu, The Protector.

[54] Qur'an, Ch.59:23.

[55] Qur'an, Ch.87:1-4.

[56] Qur'an, Ch.2:164.

[57] Qur'an, Ch.59:23.

[58] Qur'an, Ch.64:3.

[59] Qur'an, Ch.36:83.

[60] Qur'an, Ch.20:82.

[61] Qur'an, Ch.12:39-40.

[62] Qur'an, Ch.3:8.

[63] See The Psalms of Islam: Al-Sahiffat al-Sajjaddiyyah,Tr.Willliam C. Chittick, The Muhammadi Trust, London, 1988), p.227.

[64] The belief in Islam is that God sent 124,000 messengers to all nations in their own languages. Of these, Muslims believe in all the biblical prophets and consider Prophet Muhammad to be the final of all the prophets for the Message got completed with him. The message that all prophets brought was a universal message that worship belong only to One God, Allah. This life is only a temporary sojourn at the end of which all must die and await in purgatory for the Day of Resurrection when accounting will be taken of the earthly life and mankind will face either the eternal bliss or condemnation in the Fire of Hell.

[65] Qur'an, Ch.3:189-194.

[66] Qur'an, Ch.6:59.

[67] Qur'an, Ch.2:255.

[68] Shirk is idolatry and is considered in Islam a major sin. Getting attached to worldly things to the extent that one is enslaved by them is one form of idolatry in Islam. One of the fundamental beliefs in Islam is that human beings are born free and their only slavery is to Allah. Next to the obedience to Allah the love and respect is for parents, kith and kin, neighbors, the community and also compassion and love for all mankind.

[69] Qur'an, Ch.3:26.

[70] Qur'an, Ch.2:186.

[71] Qur'an, Ch.2:110.

[72] Qur'an, Ch.16:90.

[73] Qur'an, Ch.64:4.

[74] Qur'an, Ch.18:58.

[75] Sunnah simply means the traditions of Prophet Muhammad.

[76] Qur'an, Ch.18:49.

[77] Qur'an, Ch.18:109.

[78] Qur'an, Ch.31:27.

[79] Qur'an, Ch.6:59.

[80] Qur'an, Ch.99:6-8.

[81] Qur'an, Ch.42:11.

[82] Qur'an. Ch.18:110.

[83] Qur'an, Ch.17:70.

[84] See Sheikh Tosun B. al-Halveti, The Most Beautiful Names, (Threshold Books, Vermont, U.S.A., 1985),pp.110-112.

[85] Qur'an, Ch.24:35.

[86] Qur'an, Ch.55:26-27.

[87] Qur'an, Ch.19:40.

[88] The true Messiah in the Jewish tradition must build the Third Temple. See Ezekiel, 37:26-8; Isaiah, 43: 5-6.

[89] The Messiah will also gather Jews to Israel. See Isaiah, 2: 14.

[90] Zachariah, 14:9.

[91] See www.iash.com.

[92] See Isaiah, 2: 1-4; 32:13-18: 60:15-18; Jeremiah, 31: 33-34.

[93] See www.iash.com.

[94] The Quran refers to Jesus as `Isa ibn Maryam (Jesus, Son of Mary). Actually, his proper name was `Isa (in Arabic), or Esau (in Hebrew); classical Yeshua, Latinized in the West as 'Jesus'. Neither the "J" nor the second "s" in the name Jesus is to be found in the original tongue—they are not found in the Semitic languages. The word is very simply "E S A U" a very common Jewish name, used more than sixty times in the Hebrew Bible in "Genesis". See Islam.thetruecall.com/modules.php . . .

[95] Qur'an, 19:30-3.

[96] Qur'an, 19:34-6.

[97] It is interesting to note that there is no record in the history I found in my research showing Muslims organizing, simply out of hate, burning of the revealed scriptures of other faiths. This is because of the fundamental requirement in the Qur'an upon Muslims to believe in the previously revealed scriptures and to believe in all biblical prophets. See Qur'an, 2:1-5; 2:285.

[98] Qur'an, 43:61.

[99] Qur'an, 2:136.

[100] Qur'an, 3:59-60.

[101] Qur'an, 19:36.

[102] Qur'an, 61:3. 'Ahmad' is the superlative form of the name 'Muhammad', referring to the praised status of the Prophet Muhammad.

[103] It is interesting to note that Muslims believe Jesus will return in the Last Days when the Mahdi will also appear. Jesus will confirm Mahdi to be the True Representative of the Final Message of God to mankind brought by the Prophet Muhammad. Jesus will help the Mahdi and together they will fight the Dajjal (Antichrist) to establish the Kingdom of God in which there is total peace, social justice and worship of only Allah. Dajjal will be defeated.

[104] Qur'an, 5:116-7.

SELECT BIBLIOGRAPHY

Abdullah Yusuf Ali, *The Qur'an Translation* (Toronto, 2009).

Al-Halveti, Sheikh Tosun B., *The Most Beautiful Names* (Vermont, 1985).

Al-Muzaffar, Muhammad Rida, *The Faith of Shi`a Islam* (London, 1982).

Armstrong, Karen, *Muhammad: A Prophet of Our Time* (New York, 2007).

—*Muhammad, A Biography of a Prophet* (New York, 1992).

Ar-Radi al-Musawi, as-Sayyid A. M., *Imam Ali: Nahj al-Balagha Sermons, Sayings and Letters* (Tehran, 1971).

At-Tabatabai, Sayyid Muhammad Husayn, *Al-Mizan: An Exegesis of the Qur'an* (Tehran, 1983).

Ayoub, Muhammad, *Islam: Faith and History,* (London, 2004).

Boa, Kenneth Dr., www.kenboa.org.

Chittick, William (Tr.)., *The Psalms of Islam: Al-Sahiffat al-Sajjaddiyyah,* (London, 1988).

Diffinbaugh, Robert, *Let Me See Thy Glory: A Study of the Attributes of God* (Texas, 1997).

Esposito, John L.; Fasching, Darrel J. and Lewis Todd, *World Religions Today* (New York, 2009).

Lau, D. C., *Confucius: The Analects* (England, 1979).

Lings, Martin, *Muhammad: His Life Based on Earliest Sources* (2006).

Muhammad Abdu Rauf, *Imam Ali Ibn Abi Talib: The First Intellectual Muslim Thinker* (1996).

Nelson, Thomas and Sons, *The Holy Bible. Revised Standard Version, Catholic Edition* (London, 1966).

Shomali, Mohammad Ali (Ed)., *God: Existence and Attributes* (London, 2008).

Tozer, A. W., *The Knowledge of the Holy* (New York, 1961).

Warren Tony, *"Bible Studies on the Attributes of God"* in www. mountainretreatorg.net/bible.html.

Selected internet citations include:

dictionary.reference.com/browse/God.

www.allaboutgod.com.

www.iash.com.

www.kenboa.org.

INDEX